CONTENTS

Games Pets Play is not only a delightful and amusing read, it is also a thoughtful and fascinating examination of the complex relationships humans 'enjoy' with their pets.

Bruce Fogle maintains that the relationship between man and dog, for instance, is based on a fundamental misunderstanding. Whereas dogs see their humans as leaders of the pack – a straightforward submission-dominance pattern – humans tend to treat their pets as furry people, be they children, substitute parents, transitional objects, or a mixture of characters. We are offended if they do not conform to human codes of behaviour, by sniffing guests in embarrassing places, for instance, or eating unmentionable things. Despite this misunderstanding, pets are still good for us: they are a constant factor in our lives, always there, always ready to listen; they are non-judgmental, non-interventive; and whoever you are, they love you and, above all, they need you. The relationships people have with their pets are among the most complicated, important and rewarding of their lives.

The Author, a Canadian-born vet, has observed many pets and many pet-owners since he arrived in London on a scholarship to Regents Park in 1970 . . . and stayed – thanks to golden retriever Honey. In *Games Pets Play* a wide variety of his experiences, both funny and touching, are revealed.

DR BRUCE FOGLE

GAMES PETS PLAY

or How Not to be Manipulated by Your Pet

Illustrations by Kwill

A Methuen Paperback

First published in 1986
by Michael Joseph Ltd
This paperback edition published in 1987
by Methuen London Ltd
11 New Fetter Lane, London EC4P 4EE
Copyright © by Bruce Fogle 1986
Illustrations copyright © by Kwill 1986
Made and printed in Great Britain by
Richard Clay Ltd, Bungay, Suffolk

British Library Cataloguing in Publication Data

Fogle, Bruce
  Games pets play, or, How not to be
  manipulated by your pet.
  1. Pets – Social aspects
  I. Title
  636.08′87   SF411.5

ISBN 0-413-14330-9

DEDICATION

I met Michael McCulloch in 1979. Mike was a psychiatrist born in the Midwest United States and practising in Portland, Oregon, and I was a veterinary surgeon born in Ontario and practising in London, England. Along with nine other professionals we got together at the University of Dundee in Scotland for three days to discuss, for the first time, the relationship between people and pets.

We were both the same age. That always helps a friendship. We both had full families, and that helps too, although Mike had more children and pets than me.

Our friendship started off as a professional one: he helped me to understand – he *taught* me to understand – what goes on in a veterinary practice, what role the veterinary surgeon actually plays, but our friendship became extra-professional and we corresponded and talked about other matters.

I think what appealed to me the most was that Mike was the guy next door – easy to talk to – but beneath that was a sensitive and alert mind, a compassionate mind, and the professional training of a psychiatrist.

A few years later, my wife and I took Mike and his wife Jane to see the musical *Cats* when we were all in Vienna. In the musical there is a cat, Grizabella, who is rejected by the others – an 'outcat'. Near the end of the show she sings her lament, 'Memories'. The other cats are moved by her sadness and one of them reaches out and touches Grizabella. Then the others tentatively move a little closer and they touch her and console her too. I remember catching a glimpse of Mike in that theatre at that moment and seeing him smiling – beaming really – and seeing tears running down his face.

Mike McCulloch died suddenly last year, at the hands of someone he was trying to help. I still can't help feeling angry. He was such a good man. Some of the royalties from the sale of each copy of this book are being donated to the Michael McCulloch Memorial Fund, a charitable fund set up to promote a greater understanding of the relationship between people and their pets, and the book is dedicated with warmth and affection to his wife Jane and to their children.

ACKNOWLEDGEMENTS

The author and publishers gratefully acknowledge permission to quote from the following copyright material:

Tom Blakely: Extract from column in the *Toronto Star*. Copyright © Tom Blakely.

Robert Frost: 'The Span of Life', from *The Poetry of Robert Frost*, edited by Edward Connery Lathem, published by Jonathan Cape Ltd. Reprinted by permission of the Estate of Robert Frost.

Richard Joseph: 'A Letter to the Man Who Killed My Dog'. Reprinted by permission of W. H. Allen & Co. plc.

Edgar Klauber: 'On Buying a Dog' from *Good Dog Poems*, published by Charles Scribner's & Sons. Copyright © Edgar Klauber.

Eugene O'Neill: 'Blemie's Will'. Copyright © Yale University Library.

John Steinbeck: *Travels with Charley*. Reprinted by permission of William Heinemann Ltd.

The Times: Article entitled 'Miaow Costs Youth £100'. Copyright © Times Newspapers.

E. B. White: 'The Care and Training of a Dog' from *One Man's Meat*. Copyright © 1941 E. B. White.

While every attempt has been made to contact all copyright holders, it has not always been possible and the author and publishers would be glad to rectify any errors in future reprints.

GAMES PETS PLAY

or How Not to be Manipulated by Your Pet

CHAPTER ONE

Why Pets Play Games

1. INTRODUCTION

Have you ever wondered how they know what to do, when they are taken for a saunter in the park, how they determine who are the villains and who are the good guys? I practise veterinary medicine a stone's throw from Hyde Park, dog heaven for London's canine crowd, and I'm still always amazed at how all these dogs – strangers to each other –

manage to co-exist, how they suss out each other's motives, how they know when to go up to a total stranger and say, 'Please may I play with you,' and how they know when not to.

I had slipped out of the clinic for a break, a walk in Hyde Park down to the Serpentine and back one lunchtime, when I was propositioned by a blonde. She had sparkling eyes and a sincere manner and she came right up to me and touched me. I didn't recognise her at first because I was used to seeing her with a ball in her mouth. That was a ritual game that this yellow Labrador named Daffodil always played. Daffy was a retriever but living in the heart of the city there was nothing proper to retrieve and so her retrieving instinct had been ritualised into carrying a ball. She also carried it for security and was never without it when she was brought into the clinic to see me.

Daffy wasn't much of a mixer; she liked human company more than canine company and whenever another dog came over to say hello she instantly sat down and denied the stranger access to the hidden bits. Dogs say hello to each other by sticking their noses up each other's bums. Most owners hate the thought that their dogs can be so 'crude' and 'primitive' and reprimand their pets when they do it, but that's also why dogs that are large enough are always nosing the visitors to their owner's homes!

The other reason I hadn't recognised Daffy was that I had forgotten that she had been pregnant and now she looked more like a sow than a bitch. She was heavy with milk and had stem-to-stern udder that swung when she walked.

I was dying to see the litter and managed to get myself invited back to Daffy's home to see them. That wasn't really difficult. Most pet owners look on their pets as members of the family and Mrs Henderson, Daffy's owner, was no exception. She told me she felt like a grandparent who had had nine grandchildren at once.

We started walking back, Daffy obediently following, off her lead, when she eyed a bicycle and rider on a distant path. Suddenly this Mother-Earth, this gentle, loving creature, was transformed. The hair on her back stood on end and her tail and ears shot up sending out semaphore signals – HATE! – HATE! She woofed a deep, gutteral werewolf woof that seemed to come out of her prehistoric past. There was murder in her eyes and death in her heart. Mrs Henderson leaned down and stroked Daffy and said, 'Naughty girl, you should not do that;' kissing her on the head.

Daffy was playing an aggression game, 'I hate bicycles'. She probably didn't know why, because that game too had become a ritual but – and this is most important – what I was seeing was a very simple, everyday example of how a pet can get away with acting in a manner that a responsible parent would never allow in his or her own children; how a pet can play games with its owner and win.

Just before we left Hyde Park, at the Bayswater Road side, we came to the bridle path, and as we approached it Mrs Henderson called Daffy over and put her lead on. 'She's disgusting,' I was told. 'I feed her fresh meat every day but she still wants to eat the horses' manure.' An eating game!

When we got back to Mrs Henderson's flat Daffy immediately went to her pups and stood in the middle of them and counted them. It certainly looked like she was counting them because for the first minute she looked quizzical, then she licked each one's bottom in turn. With rolecall finished she leapt out of the whelping pen, walked over to her water bowl and had a drink. On the water bowl were inscribed the words 'Always Faithful'.

Mrs Henderson went in to the kitchen to make me a cup of coffee. Her flat was immaculate and clean, everything shiny and dusted and in its right place. The sofa, however, had to be seen to be believed. It looked as if Robin Hood and his band of Merrye Men had used it for twenty years of target practice. It was in shreds, and the shredding machine was lying on it.

George was a quiet tortoiseshell cat that I had first met when she had been brought in to be castrated and had been sent home having had a hysterectomy. By then she was used to her name and from that time on, when friends questioned the choice of such a masculine name for a female cat, Mr and Mrs Henderson had replied that she was named after George Sand.

As I was about to sit on the sofa Mrs Henderson came out of the kitchen. 'Oh, don't sit there,' I was told, 'we've given that sofa to Daffy and George.'

George's destruction of the sofa and Daffy's hatred of bicycles are far from rare games and veterinary surgeons are always being asked for advice on matters like these. But sofa-destruction and bicycle-hating games don't just involve pet behaviour. Pet owner behaviour is also involved. Until quite recently, however, there has been a barrier to any real study of the behaviour of either pets or their owners. First of all, pets and their owners are in our own back garden. Science is elitist and prefers to study esoteric subjects, not why some dogs are so possessive about their owners' smelly slippers. And until recently it was unlikely that pet dog behaviour would be studied at all unless the dogs were the pets of some declining

tribe of South American Indians who shared their hammocks, their foods and their diseases with their dogs. Pet cat behaviour is still misunderstood and it is only in the last ten years that it has really been investigated at all.

Human behaviour in relation to domestic pets just wasn't exciting enough for the psychologists either: to use the prevailing scientific term, the subject wasn't 'sexy' enough. A pet owner's response to his or her pet is sentimental, frequently even gooey, and science likes to investigate more profound emotions.

But the emotional response that so many people have to their pets *is* a profound emotion. It is so deep that sometimes the irrational response overwhelms the rational. We need to understand these responses that we have to our pets before we can understand why pets play the games that they do with us, or, more specifically, why we let them get away with what they do. To understand all of this we need a little knowledge of dog and cat behaviour and also of human behaviour. In what follows I am going to refer mostly to dogs, simply because there is more known about their behaviour than of other domestic animals. Most of the animal stories that I will tell will be dog stories. The pet owner stories, however, the stories that recount how pet owners behave, apply almost equally to cat owners and dog owners.

2. ANIMAL BEHAVIOUR

Ben is a sleepy-eyed, laconic two-year-old Cocker Spaniel with a tuft of pale blond puppy hair on the top of his head that never fell out. Ben sleeps on his owners' bed.

Ben's sleeping arrangements aren't that unusual. Over half of all the dog and cat owners in Britain and North America probably let their pets sleep in their bedrooms and lots of these pets sleep on their owners' beds, or even under the covers. The difference with Ben is that he doesn't allow his owners to sleep with him! Each night when he sees them getting ready for bed, he jumps on to it and watches them. If they even look at him, he gives the Cocker Spaniel version of moving furniture, that deep unremitting rumble. He stares at his owners directly – eyeball to eyeball. He purses his lips. And when they reach for the covers, he snaps.

Don't snore, darling, you'll wake the dog

When Ben first started behaving like this he was just shoved off the bed. But Ben persevered. He took up a new position under the bed and continued his cement mixer impression. Any bit of visible flesh was fair game, although basically he was an ankle man.

Ben is still one of my patients, so I know him pretty well. Ben's owners are a professional couple in their early thirties, a couple of earnest high achievers who dress in the obligatory serious suits of their financial professions. Ben was purchased as a stop-gap to parenthood. Both owners are career building and a family is being postponed, perhaps indefinitely.

Now, in spite of Ben's fierce, even odious, behaviour at home, his owners still adore him. During the day he is taken to work and is a good companion, playful with strangers. Unlike many other Golden Cocker Spaniels, he never gives me any worries when I examine him. He will let me open his mouth, check his tonsils, clean out his ears or lip folds or manipulate any of his other bits. He just looks at me in a droll way or turns away and looks into the middle distance, avoiding conflict and not giving the least indication of trouble. But each night around midnight, this Cocker goes primitive and becomes Mr Hyde.

Ben's behaviour is influenced by several variables. At its base, it is influenced by his genetic make-up, by the genes that dictate his basic social instincts. The canine species has survived because, among other things, its members have always instinctively defended their dens. Perhaps that's all that Ben is doing.

Secondly, pet behaviour is 'imprinted' into the young animal by its mother. This imprinting occurs in the first few weeks of life and influences behavioural characteristics like the need for contact or barking. Ben's mother might have imprinted his antisocial behaviour on him.

A pet's behaviour is also influenced by the experience it gains from both its mother and its littermates. Learning how to behave with other dogs, learning the limits when play gets too rough, for example, is done from experience. But Ben isn't living with other dogs now. His pack are people and he has never learned exactly what their social needs are, so he's willing to test them to the maximum.

The final influence on pet behaviour is selective breeding. This is, of course, what separates all the domestic species from the others. Through our intervention we selectively breed pets for certain characteristics, for retrieving, for docility, for protectiveness, and by accident for such negative characteristics as heart disease and cancer or, in the case of English Golden Cocker Spaniels like Ben, a Dr Jekyll/Mr Hyde syndrome. We alter the genetic array and, by doing this, alter and influence the behaviour of our pets and the games that they play. Cocker Spaniels were originally bred to retrieve woodcocks from dense underbrush, but in the 1920s they became fashionable as house pets and the blond variety became particularly popular. The breed was created for one purpose but is now used for a completely different one. Sometimes that doesn't work.

In each game that I recount I will describe the game from the pet's point of view and from the pet owner's point of view. Ben is in fact playing several games. He's playing a territory game, 'Get lost, buster. I'm in charge here' (see p. 102). He's playing a dominance game, 'Simon says . . .' (see p. 114). He might also be playing a jealousy game. 'Pay attention to me' (see p. 144), or the ritual game, 'Don't ask me why I do it, I just do it' (see p. 164).

Ben's owners are also playing games. It certainly seems so from the solution they found to their problem, a solution that was to them practical and eliminated the nightly confrontation. They moved into their spare room. They told me this almost in passing, certainly with no malice borne towards the dog when he was brought into the clinic for a routine booster inoculation. Their games are just as intriguing and just as complicated as Ben's are.

3. AN EXPLANATION OF GAMES

Before I get to the actual games themselves, I had better explain some of the words that I am going to use. It'll be short. I promise.

First of all, when I use the word 'game' I don't mean ball games or playing games. When I was a veterinary student in the early 1960s, Dr Eric Berne, a psychologist, wrote a thoughtful and interesting book called *Games People Play*. In that book, Berne developed his theories on how we can analyse our behaviour with other people in order to understand the deeper reasons for why we behave the way we do. He called our behaviour with each other 'transactions' and the subject came to be called 'transactional analysis'. A transaction can also be called a game.

According to Berne, games are basically dishonest because they are played for ulterior motives. Each game has a gimmick or a pay-off. If we disregard psychosomatic illness in pets for the moment (such things as feigned lameness), then technically I shouldn't really use the word 'game' to describe a pet's behaviour because there aren't any gimmicks in their games. Pets play games with us simply to reinforce their role and place in the social order of the home or, from their point of view, within the pack. The games that pets play may be healthy or unhealthy – you may agree or disagree with Ben the Cocker's behaviour – but basically they are honest games.

The games that people play with their pets, on the other hand, can genuinely be called 'games' because they are often played for an ulterior reward or pay-off other than the obvious

There, there, did the nasty man taste bitter then?

one. When a pet owner picks up a little yapper and scolds it for being such a groveller, outwardly the owner is dominating the dog and telling it to be quiet, but he is also getting his own hidden reward from the exercise – physical contact with a warm furry object.

A dog's basic behaviour is commonly shared by other members of the canine family and has been most studied in wolf packs. A dog is programmed to be submissive to those with higher status, to prefer not to be alone, to howl or bark in order to rally its pack and to gorge itself and vomit easily. A dog needs to work off excess energy and gets bored and frustrated with idleness, needs to use its brain and wants its pack leader's approval unless it already is the pack leader.

Dogs play games in order to maintain their position in the pack, to maintain their social stability (or, to use the technical word, their homeostasis), to reinforce their social position or to improve it. They play their games in order to maintain their psychological equilibrium or, as the psychologist would say, to get 'strokes'. In this context getting 'stroked' does not mean getting petted. A 'stroke' is an act of recognition. When you say 'Good dog' to your resident canine you are 'stroking' it in a psychological sense and I will use this term when I describe actual games.

Dogs develop fixed positions very early in life, many before they are twelve weeks old, and they maintain these positions in order to get 'stroked – to receive recognition. The way dogs do this is through developing rituals with their owners. Dogs love rituals, and feeding, greeting and sleeping rituals are the most common. Ben's defence of his owners' bed is partly a ritual through which he maintains his position, gets 'stroked' and receives recognition.

Although we selectively breed dogs to emphasise certain traits and characteristics, for example German Shepherds to protect or Labradors to be gentle-mouthed, through the games we play with them we sometimes sow the seeds of a lifetime's odious habits the day we bring a new pet home.

Many of these habits develop, not because of a lack of care or attention from the owner – in many cases the training is textbook perfect, it's just that the wrong textbook has been used – the habits develop because the pet is treated as, and is thought to respond like, a human, rather than a dog or a cat. This is fundamental to many of the games that people play with their pets.

A few months ago, a publican brought his Rottweiler into the clinic to be destroyed. It had attacked his wife two weeks previously and she was still in the hospital. That day it had attacked his daughter. As I got things ready he said, 'It's funny, you know. I didn't choose him. He chose me.' As my nurse held up a front leg and raised the vein, and as I injected the overdose of barbiturate, he continued, crying, 'He ran straight to me and played with me. He chose me.'

The publican had his own reasons for choosing this dog

Good boy, Floppy. Now let Mrs Perkins say hello as well

over the others in the litter and his reasons wouldn't be unusual. Many of us are enchanted by the self-confident pup that bounds up to us and greets us. I certainly am. 'I'm so much fun you must take me home,' they seem to be saying. They're fluffy and cute and their pugnaciousness is laughable because of their size. But they grow. And these are the pups that through their genes and their imprinting and their early interactions with their littermates, are programmed to be leaders. They are the boss dogs, the most dominant ones. I've stopped telling owners of this type of pup that they've bought a natural leader. Rather than resulting in the owner paying more attention to proper training, the comment instils in most of them a feeling of pride. They play 'Look. I'm a lion tamer', until the problems begin. The Rottweiler, in attempting to reassert his standing in his pack by attacking other members, by doing something that in a wolf pack would have led to eventual leadership, hadn't either learned or been taught the rules of the games people play and instead signed his own death warrant.

4. INSTINCT AND CULTURE

The psychology of pet behaviour is simple in comparison to the psychology of pet owner behaviour. How do you explain how an apparently uncomplicated, stable, secure thirty-year-old couple will move out of their bedroom – actually give it up to their dog – because the dog growls at them? There are reasons why people behave like this, why so many pet owners act so irrationally with their pets, but many of these reasons are buried deep in our biological or cultural past.

Let me try to explain. Biologically speaking our past survives in us in the very deepest core of our being. Evolution is like adding layers to an onion. The outer layer contains the most recent adaptations but the inner layers were laid down millions of years ago. And if you peel off enough layers, if you get to the very heart of the onion, you eventually reach the very beginning – the creation of life. Be it dog, cat, human or other, each act of creation, between fertilisation and birth, briefly re-enacts the whole of evolution. We can look at this in another way too; what we call our instinctive responses are really biological responses that emanate from our ancestral core of knowledge. To our primitive ancestors, for example, the sight of sleeping animals was a safety signal meaning that they weren't about to be attacked by another marauding tribe or eaten by sabre-toothed tigers. Which is why so many people today allow their pets to sleep in their bedrooms.

Our instinctive responses are deep down, biological responses but our cultural responses have all been created since the human moved out of the cave and jungle and became urban and agricultural.

Let me give you an example. Pauline Fisher's dog Gareth is a real nuisance – a bore. He lives on the fifteenth floor of a tower block and bites everyone who enters the flat. He also tries to bite every dog he sees when he is taken out for his exercise. He tries to bite me when I examine him and that's why I think he's such a jerk. Gareth is a Welsh Corgi and Pauline has one because she was brought up with Corgis and so was her mother. In fact, before her family moved to London, they always had Corgis. The Fishers don't know what to do about Gareth's bloodlust and I can't help them too much. I can, however, explain how they came to have such an inappropriate pet in a tower block in London.

Our cultural traditions can date back thousands of years or they might come from the last decade. Often, these cultural traditions can be buried and forgotten in our past but still set the rules for the games we play today.

In European culture, the ruling classes were the first people to breed hunting dogs and certainly the first to breed lap dogs. In any culture, it is only a matter of time before the masses want to emulate the powerful; to be more like them. The psychologist would call it 'identification'. And so the lower classes, in wanting to identify with their influencers, in wanting to incorporate into their lives something seen to be valuable, also started keeping more domestic pets. In other cultures, the Chinese for instance, there is no history of using dogs in hunting, which is why they don't keep dogs as pets. We have a history of our leaders keeping pets, which is one of the reasons why our leaders today still find it so important to be seen to keep pets (every American president has his picture taken with his pet) and which is also why Pauline Fisher and the rest of us have been culturally influenced to keep dogs.

But why a Corgi? In the 1930s, Pauline's grandmother got a Corgi as a pet because for some obscure reason the Royal Family had taken on these powerful little dogs as pets. Pauline's grandmother was identifying with the Royal Family. And so Pauline is stuck with a tough cattle dog on the fifteenth floor of a high rise in the middle of the city today because of an act of identification by her grandparents fifty years ago.

5. PETS AS PEOPLE

The psychology of games is influenced by our culture but it is also strongly influenced by our tendency to see pet behaviour and actions in human terms, to anthropomorphise.

Several years ago I had the opportunity to attend a scientific symposium in Vienna, held in honour of the Nobel Prize winner Konrad Lorenz on his eightieth birthday. When Dr Lorenz spoke he told us how he first became interested in animal behaviour, the study of which led to his receiving the Nobel Prize for Medicine. He told us about a duck that he had raised when he was six years old, from hatching onwards. He didn't know anything about imprinting then, and didn't know that the duck thought that Lorenz was his mother, but he told us that he instinctively understood the meaning of the duck's different sounds. 'I understood the "weeping" of that duck,' he told us, 'and I quacked. I swear I do remember that duck stopped weeping and changed its sound to the greeting sound.' It was a marvellous story to hear from Dr Lorenz himself – but he was anthropomorphising.

As a result of Lorenz's original work we now know a lot more about communication between animals, but there is still so much that is inexplicable. I'm always amazed at how perceptive some owners can be. When my old Retriever, Honey, was in her later years she suffered a few mild strokes. On two occasions, the day before a stroke, my wife said, 'There's something wrong with Honey.' On each occasion I examined the dog thoroughly, ran blood profiles and exercise tests, and could find nothing specific. I asked Julia if she could pinpoint anything in particular but she couldn't. 'All I know is that she's not herself,' she replied.

My wife was unconscious of the specific behavioural changes that Honey was showing but she was exquisitely sensitive to them. Dogs, however, are experts in this area and rapidly learn to respond to the subtlest forms of communication: the slope of a shoulder, the raising of an eyebrow, a suitcase in a different place. Dogs play their subtlest games when communication is refined down to virtually symbolic moves.

We give our pets non-verbal signals when we act in any ways that are different from the norm. *We* might not realise we are acting differently but our pets certainly do. Non-verbal communication is important and once we accept that it is, we can accept anthropomorphism.

Science is critical of anthropomorphism but in some ways we're not anthropomorphic enough. If Goofy is dressed in clothes, if Snoopy has anxiety attacks, if Bambi panics when his mother is caught in the forest fire, I think it's terrific. It's terrific because it teaches us that animals feel, behave and suffer rather like us. Most higher mammals share basic signals to convey pain, fear, anger, joy and surprise. When I look at a cat that has been in a road traffic accident it doesn't have to tell me how it feels, I read fear or pain in its eyes. We share these methods of communication with other animals and when it comes to expressing our deepest feelings, our profoundest emotions, we usually revert back to non-verbal behaviour: an embrace, a pat on the shoulder, a clasping of hands, a squeeze, a glance.

Professional writers have always been fascinated by the signals that a dog can send with its eyes. James Thurber wrote that, 'The eyes of the sensitive poodle can shine with such an unalloyed glee, and darken with so profound a gravity as to disconcert the masters of the earth who have lost the key to so many of the simpler magics.' Thurber never lost that key and played 'catch me if you can' games with his dog right to the end of his life. Konrad Lorenz didn't either. He described how he acquired one of his dogs this way. 'Quivering with consternation and with his tail between his legs, he stood at a safe distance saying with his eyes, "I'll do anything at all for you – except leave you." ' Pets are quite sophisticated with the signals they send us. We, of course, interpret these signals in our own way, and this is where anthropomorphism goes wrong.

Cat owners, for example, are constantly telling me that their cats scratch furniture to gain attention. They don't. They almost always do it to groom their claws, but lots of owners feel guilty about not spending enough time with their cats, or leaving them at home alone during the day, and they persist in thinking that their cats are 'getting back at them'.

Even more frequently people will tell me that they keep warning their dogs not to pee on curtains or rape cushions or eat so quickly but that their pets pay no attention. Owners forget that dogs are dogs and although they can understand quite a few words in English or any other language, they leave school before they learn to cope with conditional clauses like, 'I'll rub your nose in it if you do it again!' Many pet owners feel that their pets understand morality and aesthetics. 'He only does it to annoy me,' I'm told, or, 'She did it to get even.'

Most people treat their pets as members of the family, as entities that are not quite as 'animal' as the rest of the animal world. James Thurber, once again, put it clearly when he said of his poodle, Christabel, 'She is not a hunter or a killer but an interested observer of the life of the lower animals of which she does not consider herself one.'

Looking upon pets as members of the family helps to explain why so many pet owners are convinced that their dogs will die of starvation unless they are fed very specific diets. Ten years ago on short notice, I took in John Gielgud's dogs for a month while Sir John visited America. Each Wednesday the Harrods van delivered fresh duck liver pâté, fresh prawns and Swedish butter biscuits. It was a terrible diet for dogs. My family ate royally for a month.

Dogs and cats act like dogs and cats but we treat them as quasi-humans. It means that although the games they play with us are usually straightforward, the ones we play with them are far more complicated and the final complication that we should understand before we get to the actual games is how we see or use our pets as symbols.

6. PETS AS SYMBOLS

The pet's symbolic role as a child is a self-evident one but pets can also act as symbolic adults. The well-trained guide dog for the blind is the classic example. Most people see the guide dog as a mature and sensible individual who stops at each busy road, computes all the factors that are necessary (movement of traffic, colour of the lights, obstacles, where other people are crossing), shifts the information through his or her pragmatic and adult brain, and then, taking full responsibility, guides the blind owner across the road. But dogs can also act as adults in other less obvious situations.

My new dog, Liberty, is now a full-grown Golden Retriever bitch who loves to place boisterous games. I'm speaking of play in the classic sense of the word where the dog pretends to be obsessed with an emotion which she does not really feel. Libby stalks tennis balls. She also plays with her friend, a younger and smaller black dog named Tadpole, grabbing Tad by the skin of her neck and shaking her. She gives quite a growl and gives Tad a good shake but she does it with no malice; her toothhold has no pressure. She plays for the joy of playing. Similarly, she will play for minutes at a time with a grape on the floor. She makes the grape 'flee' by batting it with her paw, then chases it, corners it, and makes it 'flee' again. When she gets tired of playing that game she has a simple way of finishing it. She bolts down the grape.

I like playing games too and I play rough and tumble games with my son. I grab him from behind. I hold him and trip him backwards and drop him on to the carpet. I stand with one leg on his chest and bellow like Johnny Weissmuller. *And Liberty comes to the rescue.* That's not completely true. Ben interprets Libby's interest in the goings-on as Libby coming to his rescue. As soon as Libby hears the commotion when Ben and I have a rough and tumble, she races into the room barking. Not woofing, barking. 'Lay off him or I'll kill you!' Ben sees the dog saying to me. Ben sees his dog sizing up the situation, realising that Ben is (if you will pardon the pun) the underdog and coming to rescue him from the bully. And when we play with the tables turned, and Ben has me in a footlock, he sees Libby as coming to protect me. Ben isn't the only person who sees his pet dog playing the symbolic role of an adult, but of course all that Libby is really doing is wanting to join in the shenanigans. If she were to bite, it is just as likely that she would bite the underdog as the oppressor.

Pets also play another symbolic role, and this is the most complicated one. For many people, perhaps unconsciously for

most, a pet dog symbolically plays the role of a parent. The pet gives comfort and solace, physical contact and constancy and a loyalty unlike anything else on earth. A pet dog offers a type of dedication that, outside of infancy, we never get and never hope of getting. This is probably the most important symbolic role that pets play and it probably has the most profound effect on the psychology of pet ownership. I will discuss it in more detail under Submission Games (p. 126). It is also the most difficult one to come to terms with because it can also explain the strange ambivalence we feel towards our pets.

How is it that a pet owner can overwhelmingly love a dog, treat it as a member of the family, yet let it out on its own in the centre of London all day, to fend for itself in the traffic? On one occasion when I was taking my dog to the park, I came across a Dachshund, an obviously sensible dog, standing at a zebra crossing, waiting for a break in the traffic so that it could cross into the park. There was no one with the dog and I took it home and phoned the number on its tag. The owner exploded at my intervention and told me I should take the dog back to the zebra crossing, from which it would find its own way home. How dare I interfere with her dog's pleasure! Things got worse when she was obliged to come over to pick up the dog. When she realised that I was a veterinary surgeon she became convinced that I was really just touting for business, that I had picked up her dog in order to pick up a new client. She was incapable of understanding my concern for the safety of her dog. How could this lady love her dog and put it at such risk at the same time? Konrad Lorenz asked himself a similar question. 'If I meet a man who has just been boasting of the prowess and other wonderful properties of one of his dogs, I always ask him whether he has still got the animal. The answer then is all too often strongly reminiscent of the old adage, "No I had to get rid of him – I moved to another town – or into a smaller house – I got another job and it was awkward for me to keep a dog," or some other similar excuse. It is to me amazing that many people who are otherwise morally sound feel no disgrace in admitting such action.'

This ambivalent attitude even exists in the words we use for our pets. When I was at high school, a 'dog' was the last person you ever wanted to be seen on a date with. Girls who were 'catty' were only marginally better than girls who were 'bitchy' and neither were near the top of the list. The words indicated contempt or spite or maliciousness. They all had negative connotations. But at the same time, I really loved my dog and my cat. I thought they were gorgeous and gentle and beautiful. They were faithful and loyal and loved me in return.

In my practice today I see my clients living the same dichotomy but in a different way. 'Don't worry, he'd never bite,' they say as the dog snarls and drools and stares me straight in the eye giving me the double whammy. People are amazingly defensive and protective of their pets, to a degree that does suggest that they are playing a symbolic role for the owner.

The loyalty that people attribute to their dogs is a fiction. The utter devotion, absolute trust, overwhelming love, unending adoration – all of these things are in the minds of the owners, not in the minds of the dogs. The dogs are behaving as good pack members, maintaining their positions in the pack by doing things that all good pack members *should* do: rally the pack to intruders, protect the den from outsiders, assist in the hunt for food, expose the undercarriage in submission, acquiesce to grooming to denote a lower status in the pecking order. Dogs have their own social reasons for acting the way they do but we have our own reasons for interpreting their behaviour in a symbolic fashion.

There are rational reasons for the games pets play and there are irrational ones. There are also rational and irrational reasons for pet owner behaviour. The veterinary surgeon probably hears more of these stories or sees more apparently crazy behaviour than anyone else. Some people tell me I see lots of crazy behaviour because I practise right in the middle of London and, because that's such a crazy place to live, I see lots of people who are genuinely crazy. Relief veterinary surgeons who work in my practice frequently describe my clients as 'tricky' or 'difficult'. I've never experienced anything else so I consider them to be quite normal. But there might be a point to what I am told.

Who loves his mummy more
than anybody or anything
in the whole wide world, then?

An extremely urban area like central London will undoubtedly attract a certain type of person who will keep certain types of pets and behave with them in certain ways. That means that what I see each day, and the games I am going to describe to you, might make sense in London or Montreal or New York but make no sense at all in Waltham-on-the-Wolds or Moose Jaw or Centerville. As you read further, it is worth remembering what Mohave Dan, a desert hermit who lived with a colony of dogs, once told the writer J. Allen Boone. 'There's facts about dogs and there's opinions about them,' he said. 'The dogs have the facts and humans have the opinions. If you want facts about a dog, always get them straight from the dog. If you want opinions get them from humans.'

CHAPTER TWO

Social Games

1. ATTACHMENT GAMES

PET: 'FORGIVE ME. I'M ONLY HUMAN'

The dog was a mess – a real mess. It had dragged itself into John and Marilyn's garden that morning, and by noon the Jenkinses were back in London seeing me, having given up their week in the country. Maggots performed slow motion undulations in the deep wound in the dog's thigh. Grease and dry caked blood covered most of his body. He was worn and dehydrated, but he gave me the same signals he had given the Jenkinses. 'I won't complain,' he said with his eyes, 'but I need your help.' And I reacted in the same way the Jenkinses did.

Reggie's treatment (formal name Reject Jenkins – Reggie for short) was uncomplicated: intravenous fluids to compensate for his dehydration, and bubbling hydrogen peroxide cleansing of his wounds to flush out the livestock. With some antibiotics he was able to go home that evening.

Two days later John brought the dog back in so that I could look at the wounds and see, now that they were clean, if any of them needed stitching up. Reggie positively glided in. He investigated the examining room but constantly looked up at John – looking for cues. He was obviously a well-trained dog – a house pet who had strayed or been discarded and who had been hit by a car some days prior to his wandering into the Jenkins's garden. John told him to sit and with complete obedience Reggie did so, looking away to avoid eye contact with me as I examined his wounds.

'What are you going to do now?' I asked John. He has his own design consultancy business and didn't strike me as the type of person who would be happy with a mutt. I would have expected from the way he dressed in casual but expensive 'designer' clothes and from the car he drove, a large BMW, that if he were to have a dog at all it would be a 'designer' dog, something fashionable like a Shar-Pei or a Bichon Frise, not a black and tan mongrel of indeterminate parentage. 'I'm keeping him,' he said. 'This dog spent a fair time looking for me. Now I'm his person and he's my dog.' John Jenkins described the attachment between himself and his dog as lucidly and as simply as can be done but both the dog and the man were following their instincts for opposite reasons.

Dogs have a biological need for attachment and I have explained some of these needs in the previous chapter on why pets play games. Attachment is necessary for their survival and the instinct is there from birth; from the first successful search for a teat. But how does it come about that they choose us as attachment figures? To understand that we really have to understand basic canine behaviour.

Dogs are a social species and just the same as in other social species, hunger, sex, aggression, territory guarding and attachment behaviours are inherent characteristics of the species. It's the same with us. Time scales are different, however. Dogs mature very rapidly and almost all of their basic behaviour patterns are imprinted into them before they are twelve weeks of age. Attachment behaviour is at its most critical between the ages of six and twelve weeks, which is important for us to know because we usually acquire pups between these ages and by doing the wrong thing then, although we don't realise it at the time, we can be setting the wrong emotional tone for life.

In simple terms, if you deprive a pup of contact with other dogs when the pup is between six and twelve weeks of age, it is more likely that that pup will, when it is mature, find it difficult to behave normally with other dogs; that it will be more sociable and more attached to people. The converse is also true. If a pup or a kit is raised in the absence of people; if it isn't handled by people before it is twelve weeks old, then that animal is less likely to form the type of attachment that we want from our pets. These animals are the ones that will remain apprehensive of people. From the dog's or cat's point of view, it doesn't really matter who the attachment figure is. An extreme example would be Koko, a gorilla who has been taught to use American sign language. Several years ago, a kitten wandered into Koko's compound and Koko adopted it. In 1985, the cat was killed in a road traffic accident and Koko was devastated. Using sign language, she asked for another cat and was given one. Koko's owners chose a Manx because apparently that is what Koko described that she wanted, but they chose a six-week-old kitten because they knew that, like the last one, at that age the kitten would look upon Koko as an acceptable attachment figure.

Dogs and cats will accept human attachment figures if their exposure to people is properly timed. That's why it is so pointless in my view to capture wild or feral cats, neuter them and place them for adoption. These cats were not brought into social contact with people during that critical period up to twelve weeks of age, and with very few exceptions will never accept humans as attachment figures.

Dogs that look upon other dogs as riff-raff – as entities seemingly beneath them – are animals that did not have proper exposure to other dogs between the ages of six and twelve weeks. I used to try to get Honey, my old retriever, to play with other dogs in the park. 'You must be joking,' she said to me with her eyes and her body language. 'Them? Dogs? Do you *really* want me to act like one of them?' After

Honey died and we got Liberty I decided that this time I would have a dog that enjoyed playing with other dogs, that didn't look only upon humans as acceptable attachment figures. But a big medical problem arises here.

Every veterinary surgeon will tell you that your pet should not meet other dogs until the pup has completed its primary vaccination series against the various infectious diseases. This was bad enough when primary inoculation was completed at twelve weeks of age and the vaccine manufacturers recommended two more weeks before contact with other dogs is safe. But with the emergence of parvovirus, a serious and often lethal disease of the gastrointestinal system and bone marrow, vaccination procedure had to be revised and today dogs don't receive their final inoculation against parvovirus until they are eighteen weeks old. What do you do now? If a dog is deprived of contact with other dogs until that age you are inviting social mayhem. The country would be full of dogs that only look on people (or gorillas) as acceptable attachment figures.

I carefully disregarded the medical advice and selectively let Libby play, from the age of seven weeks when we got her, with our neighbour's German Shepherd, my sister-in-law's Bearded Collie and my mother-in-law's Norfolk Terrier. And because we live above the clinic I introduced her almost daily to other pups. The plan worked well – maybe too well. I now have a really 'doggy' dog, a dog that if given the choice between eating a steak, playing with people or playing with dogs, will play with dogs. When I take her into Hyde Park she invariably races off and finds a Dobermann or Mastiff or some other tough attachment figure, indicates her subservience, then forms a small pack with them. The result of my studied intervention is that Liberty will never be reliable in the same way that Honey was. Honey was a people dog. Her attachment and obedience was to people. Liberty is a dog dog. She responds to people and is obedient to them in the gentle way of all trained Golden Retrievers, but given the opportunity she would happily attach herself to a canine leader.

One of the reasons that we choose dogs as pets is that there appears to be in their attachment behaviour a capacity for an altruistic love, a willingness to please another without outward reward. But we also choose them because we are helplessly programmed to do so.

OWNER: 'HE NEEDS ME!'

'I wish to buy a dog,' she said,
'A dog you're sure is quite well bred.
In fact, I'd like some guarantee
He's favored with a pedigree.'

'My charming friend,' the pet man said,
'I have a dog that's so well bred,
If he could talk, I'll guarantee
He'd never speak to you or me.'

We choose pets for all sorts of reasons and our choices, as Edgar Klauber's poem suggests, reveal aspects of our personalities and our needs, in fact reveal the games *we* play.

I see dogs and cats that are kept as status symbols; flavour of the month breeds. I see others that are kept so that the owner can play 'I'm a lion tamer', walking down the street with a hulking slobbering delinquent on a chain. Others keep certain animals or breeds to give real or symbolic security, or in my case to allow me to act like a child, to be able to get down on my hands and knees and play hide and seek or tug of war and get away with it! There are countless reasons why we choose to keep pets but one of the most common is our unavoidable parenting instinct, our need to care for those who cannot care for themselves. And our pets act as parasites on us because they take advantage of our need to play 'He needs me'.

It was after two in the morning when the phone rang. My wife passed the receiver over her back and buried her head in her pillow.

'Dr Fogle! You must come immediately. Baby is having bad dreams.'

'If Baby is having bad dreams,' I muttered, 'wake him up and take him for a little walk.'

I was about to say goodnight but she continued. 'Dr Fogle, he is awake and he's having bad dreams. You must come immediately.'

I looked over and saw that Julia's visible eye was open.

'If he's awake, how can he be having bad dreams?' I asked.

Julia lifted her head from her pillow. I couldn't believe what I was hearing either.

'He is sensitive and excitable and jumps at the slightest noise. I can't do any more for him and you must come over immediately.'

'What have you done already?' I replied, by now, regrettably, wide awake.

who'd be a poorly boy without his mummy, then?

'I've given him a Valium and a Mogadon,' she answered. 'He had an upsetting day and I gave him something to calm him.'

'A whole Valium and a whole Mogadon?' I retorted. Julia's jaw was slack. She looked incredulous. 'If little Baby has had a Valium and a Mogadon I think you should just stay up with him for the rest of the night and make sure that he doesn't fall off anything and injure himself. I'm sure he will be better in twenty-four hours.'

The conversation continued . . . and continued. It finally became abrasive and for the first and one of the only times in my career, I hung up on the caller. I was being confronted with an overwhelming, perhaps pathological, attachment and I didn't know what to do. The owner was playing 'He needs me' and was trying to involve me in her game.

The episode raised a question in my mind which I still haven't answered. Should the client or the veterinary surgeon define what an emergency is? If I let the client define an emergency when I know that medically speaking it isn't one, am I by responding to her wishes helping to make that person more dependent on her pet? If I offer the service that is requested, am I reinforcing a pathological attachment? Am I helping to change the bond between pet owner and pet into bondage?

Pets, of course, have no qualms in these situations. Although they don't know it they parasitise our need to nurture. We haven't helped either because we have created many breeds of dog, Baby among them, that are 'arrested' infants for their entire lives. These dogs show absurd amounts of joy on their owner's return, hero-worship the most appalling owners and are unashamedly servile – real sycophants. They have an overwhelming dependence on humanity that dominates all of their other behaviour characteristics.

'He needs me' isn't just played by people who are emotionally dependent on their pets. My colleague Andrew Carmichael took into hospital a half-blind heart-diseased geriatric

Shih Tzu but didn't want to leave it alone at his clinic while he went windsurfing one Sunday afternoon. He felt that the dog needed him (a failing of more than one veterinary surgeon I know).

According to Andrew, he regretted his impulsive gesture from the start; the excitement of the journey almost put an end to the dog's dicky heart. Once he got to the reservoir he left the dog in his car, rolled the windows half down to keep the air fresh, donned his wetsuit and paddled out on his board. No sooner had he stood up on his surfboard than he saw this cataractous cardiac case of a dog stiffly stumbling into the water, preparing to swim out to him. He swam for all his worth, headed the dog to shore, packed up and returned to London, swearing he would never fall for the same game again.

But even the toughest fall for it. Jack London's hero John Thornton in *The Call of the Wild* was described this way:

> Other men saw to the welfare of their dogs from a sense of duty and business expediency; he saw to the welfare of

Pay no attention, he's just trying to make me feel needed

his as if they were his own children, because he could not
help it. He had a way of taking Buck's head roughly
between his hands, and resting his own head on Buck's,
of shaking him back and forth, the while calling him ill
names that to Buck were love names.

It's difficult not to fall for this game. We can find many other
outlets for our need to nurture, religious and humanitarian
ones being the most pronounced, but even Pope John Paul II
enjoys having breakfast each morning with his pet cat. Pets
parasitise our need to nurture because they fulfil by accident
roles that, through human evolution, have developed to perpetuate our parenting instinct. We are primed to feel a need for
attachment. It's central to our survival. Attachment – a feeling
of needing and of being needed – is stimulated by face, voice
and eye signals, by sharing experiences, especially happy
experiences, through dependency, responsibility and coopera-
tive behaviour, through physical contact and through pleasant
feelings that are brought on by the person you are attached to.
But dogs, because of their facial expressions and because of the
feelings we impute them to have, fill almost all of these qual-
ifications. And they do it without even uttering a word. That's
very important. Because words don't enter into it, our attachment to our pets becomes Utopian. It is unsullied by reality.

One of the best examples of this is Senator George Vest's
famous tribute to dogs. Before he became an American
senator in the middle of the last century, George Vest, a
lawyer, once represented in court a man whose dog had been
shot. Without preparation, without a legal secretary, research
assistants or piles of A4 paper, he spoke extemporaneously to
the jury. He didn't speak long but this is what he said:

> The best friend a man has in the world may turn
> against him and become his enemy. His son or daughter
> that he has reared with loving care may prove ungrateful.
> Those who are nearest and dearest to us, those whom we
> trust with our happiness and our good name, may

become traitors to their faith. The money a man has, he may lose. It flies away from him, perhaps when he needs it most. A man's reputation may be sacrificed in a moment of ill-considered action. The people who are prone to fall on their knees to do us honour when success is with us may be the first to throw the stone of malice when failure settles its cloud upon our heads.

The one absolutely unselfish friend a man can have in this selfish world, the one that never deserts him, the one that never proves ungrateful or treacherous, is his dog. A man's dog stands by him in prosperity and in poverty, in health and in sickness. He will sleep on the cold ground, where the wintry winds blow and the snow drives fiercely, if only he may be near his master's side. He will kiss the hand that has no food to offer; he will lick the wounds and sores that come in encounter with the roughness of the world. He guards the sleep of a pauper master as if he were a prince.

When all other friends have deserted, he remains. When riches take wings, and reputation falls to pieces, he is as constant in love as the sun in its journey through the heavens. If fortune drives the master forth an outcast in the world, friendless and homeless, the faithful dog asks no higher privilege than that of accompanying him, to guard him against danger, to fight against his enemies. And when the last scene of all comes, and death takes the master in its embrace and his body is laid away in the cold ground, no matter if all other friends pursue their way, there by the graveside will the noble dog be found, his head between his paws, his eyes sad but open in alert watchfulness, faithful and true even in death.

The jury adjourned for four minutes, then returned awarding five hundred dollars in damages for the dog owner although in his claim he had only asked for fifty dollars! The judge had to intervene.

Vest had struck a chord with that jury, probably all of whom had hunting dogs, and that chord is still struck today. Pet owners interpret their dog's attachment to them in their own idealistic ways. And the more intensely both the pets and their owners feel about attachment, the more varied will be the separation games that they play.

2. SEPARATION GAMES

PET: 'IF YOU LEAVE ME I'LL SCREAM'

It continued all night. My bedroom was four floors above the hospitalisation area of the clinic but I still heard it – yodelling. I had a Dobermann staying in the hospital for the night in preparation for routine surgery the following morning and she didn't stop letting me know she was there until I went down at breakfast time to see whether I had just been dreaming. The experience taught me several lessons. The first was that a Dobermann's bark was a decibel level higher than Concorde taking off. And in the dead of night it seems to be able to penetrate brick walls! My kennel room had double-glazed windows and a sound-proofed ventilation system, yet I still heard her as if she were in the next room.

It also taught me that it isn't only the grovellers that play separation games; it's not just the Yorkshire Terriers and Miniature Poodles that do it. Even 'real' dogs, German

Shepherds, Labradors and Dobermanns will sound off if they are separated from their packs. It also taught me that, regardless of the reason for a dog's noise-making, I should be more considerate to its feelings and, when the circumstances dictate it, give it one of the safe anti-anxiety drugs so that the animal has a more contented night.

Candie and Sweetie play 'If you leave me I'll scream' before they even reach the front door of the clinic. And unless my nurse, Jenny (a Barbara Woodhouse clone), shouts them into submission, they will continue until after they leave the premises. Candie and Sweetie wear collars encrusted with semi-precious stones. The dogs are bathed twice weekly and are brought in for me to see at the slightest sign of any irregularity of habits. What would justify Mrs Parsons, the owner, taking a spoonful of kaolin for herself, warrants a day off work if one of her dogs suffers a similar complaint. These dogs have been indulged all their lives and have never been taught the basics of responsible behaviour. They are hopelessly dependent on their leader, Mrs Parsons, and they show it.

Candie and Sweetie were never properly socialised, either with other dogs or with people. When they are brought in to see me they play 'If you leave me I'll scream' because they are helpless without their boss dog, who happens to be a person. 'If you leave me I'll scream' isn't the only game they play. At home they pretend they are the SAS or the Green Berets and go on search and destroy missions. Their owner complains that the dogs are still not fully housetrained. These dogs learned in puppyhood how to play games with their owners and separation games are just a part of their routine.

Mrs Parsons is a successful businesswoman, married and in her mid-thirties. I've never met Mr Parsons but assume that he exists. It is a rare event when her dogs are not with her. Candie and Sweetie are poodles, an intelligent breed, perhaps even the most intelligent of the popular breeds, and neither dog suffers from any apparent defect that would prevent them from developing into responsible and fun dogs. But these dogs learned early on how to handle their owner. Beg and crawl, make physical contact, act helpless, *whine*. Do these things and you get your rewards.

Mrs Parsons liked the begging. It made her feel she was needed. She didn't know that her dogs begged not because they loved her but because in their minds she was such an authority figure they felt they needed to be obsequious in the most slavish way. Candie and Sweetie had never been allowed to mix with other dogs. They were people dogs, screwed-up people dogs. From Mrs Parsons's viewpoint she enjoyed the satisfaction we all get from feeling needed. She was getting lots of rewards from her dogs – companionship, contact comfort and lots of licks. She was getting 'stroked'. Candie and Sweetie were of course clever, as dogs are, at learning the tricks of the trade. But they were playing 'If you leave me I'll scream' for other reasons.

Candie and Sweetie live in a cosseted protected jail of a world. Because they were isolated from other dogs when they were young they remain timid of other dogs today and hate to be in the presence of them, like when they are brought to the clinic and have to spend a few minutes in the reception room. They freak out and start screaming. The isolation that Mrs Parsons implemented when they were pups is also the reason for their hyperactivity.

The games that dogs play are learned in early experience, in that critical time up to around twelve weeks of age and this sets the baseline for the emotional development of the animal. The games that a dog learns or is taught will affect its ultimate relationship with people and with other dogs. If pups are too cosseted when they are under twelve weeks of age they suffer from stimulus hunger and simply don't make good pets. If you deprive *any* social species of emotional or sensory stimulation, it doesn't matter whether it is a rat or a human, the deprivation encourages degenerative changes to the brain and also increases the risk of organic disease and illness. Put in its simplest form, activity – touching, talking and playing with young pets – is biologically as well as psychologically good for both you and your pet. It is necessary for their proper development and helps you as well.

Although Candie and Sweetie have every toy imaginable, they spend their lives in their luxury jail deprived of stimulation, only let out on a lead to walk to the car and be driven to work, or for a short walk in the park, to 'empty their little tanks', as Mrs Parsons describes it. Mrs Parsons has a large emotional investment in these dogs and is frightened that if they are let off their leads they might be attacked 'by a dog!' Although it is impossible to convince Mrs Parsons of the fact, her dogs suffer from sensory stimulation, and that's why they have such rotten behaviour. Dogs need to follow toads quizzically across back lawns (preferably into stagnant ponds). Poodles in particular, because of their build, need to leap fences at a single bound, track snails, and compete in 400-yard dashes. They need exercise, activity, stimulation. If they don't receive any activity or, more important, if their only stimulation is permitted through direct contact with a leader figure like Mrs Parsons, then their tension builds up and is released in the unpleasant ways in which these dogs show it. Candie and Sweetie are emotional cripples. They are immature and will never develop, but it is not their fault, it is the fault of their owner.

Owner: 'But She Can't Live Without Me!'

My nurses plotted their revenge. Somehow I would receive retribution for what I had done. Somehow I would be made to pay – to suffer – for what I had caused. I had taken in Bronwyn Jones's Chihuahua Susie and life was a misery. Susie wasn't causing the misery. Bronwyn Jones was.

Susie is a sensible and gentle Chihuahua who is slightly overweight, has the physique of a large banana and breath like a stagnant pond. I've known the dog and her owner for nine years, since the dog was a pup, and four years back I first suggested that Susie needed her teeth scaled. Her owner declined the suggestion. Each time I saw Susie after that I suggested again that her teeth be scaled. The condition of her mouth declined and Mrs Jones continued to reject the idea of having her dog's teeth scaled. She didn't reject the idea for financial reasons nor did she fail to realise that her dog had a mouth like a cesspit. She did not hide the fact that visitors to her house commented on the pong in the air. Mrs Jones could simply not face the idea of leaving her dog with me for six hours. 'She'll pine so terribly without me,' I was told.

Susie's teeth continued to rot away and I continued to suggest treatment. Mrs Jones was told that she could sit with Susie in reception until it was time for me to anaesthetise the dog, that she could hold her dog while I anaesthetised it and that she would be telephoned as soon as we completed surgery and would be able to take her dog home as soon as Susie could stand up well enough to walk. But still she declined.

Eventually the crisis came. Susie's teeth had become so septic that each time she ate, each time she chewed on anything, she sent bacteria charging into her bloodstream and around her body. And when pus started dripping from her nostrils and Susie went off her food, I was reluctant to give in to her owner's needs any longer. 'Susie will die if I don't clear up the cause of the infection,' I lied to the owner. 'And you will be responsible!'

With what can mildly be called 'great reluctance' she left
Susie with us. Bronwyn Jones lives about fifteen minutes from
my clinic but ten minutes later she was on the phone,
breathless. 'How is Susie? Is she crying?' Mrs Jones was
assured by my nurse on reception duty that Susie was fine.
She was anaesthetised and I was removing the rotten teeth.
'Removing them? But I thought Dr Fogle was only going to
clear up the infection. She will hate how she looks with no
teeth!'

In the meantime I was downstairs in the 'dirty' operating
room, the operating room reserved for the unpleasant
procedures such as abscess lancing, anal gland syringing and
teeth scaling, pulling out teeth with what can only be called
deep contented satisfaction. Susie's upper canine teeth, the
eye teeth, were rotted to their roots and they were the cause of
the pus dripping from her nostrils, but her molars, the large
'chewers', were just as bad. Her teeth were so rotten that I
could have removed them with my fingers. It pleased me that
I could, in a single action, make that dog feel so much better.
But it also pleased me that I knew that I was removing every
single tooth and that I wouldn't have to fight with Bronwyn
Jones on that score again.

It didn't take long for me to finish. There was no scaling
involved, just simple extractions. Susie was put in a recovery
cage and I proceeded on to my next case. But not my nurses.
They simply couldn't get Mrs Jones off the phone. 'I'd like to
speak to Susie,' she said. 'I want her to know that I haven't
abandoned her.' It was explained that Susie was recovering
from surgery and, 'We don't really allow patients to receive
telephone calls while they are recovering from anaesthesia,'
but Mrs Jones didn't see my nurses' sense of humour and she
persisted. 'Susie won't understand why I left her. She will be
anxious and hearing my voice on the telephone will make her
feel better. She pines terribly when she is separated from me.'

I was protected from Mrs Jones but my nurses were not,
and for the rest of the morning what started out almost as a bit

*Hello, operator, this is an urgent
person-to-dog call*

of amusement became an onerous bore. I knew my nurses had
reached their limit when they transferred her umpteenth call
to me. 'She wants to speak to you,' Jenny said, abruptly.
Everybody wants to speak to me and both of my nurses,
Maxine and Jenny, are master tacticians at convincing pet
owners that it is not necessary for me to answer their
questions. They protect me and at the same time have the
satisfaction of fulfilling more responsible roles at the clinic.
But when I hear that curt 'She wants to speak to you,' I know
that one or the other is at breaking point; that they are about
to be driven around the twist by either an insurance salesman
or an overwrought 'mother', both of whom use the same
methods of repetitive, persistent, unremitting persuasion.

Mrs Jones was on the line. 'I know she's not going to live. I
must speak to her.' Maxine and Jenny are both better at
talking to 'anxious parents' than I am. The fact that they had
given up and passed her on to me was my cue. 'Come in, Mrs
Jones, and you can stay in the kennel room with Susie while
she recovers.' I was accepting defeat. Mrs Jones was stronger
than all of us. But I was clearing our telephone line and letting
my nurses get on with their other business.

Bronwyn Jones says that her dog can't bear to be parted from her because Bronwyn Jones can't bear to be parted from her dog. She loves her dog madly and has made a tremendous emotional investment in that dog and if that investment is threatened through separation she can suffer from sorrow, anxiety and, as she showed in a few of her phone calls, anger.

Some people are simply born to be more caring than others. Some people can feel love and suffer intensely for every living thing on earth. I'm quite certain that the act of pet ownership is a manifestation of that caring instinct; that pet owners are that part of the population who need to 'care' the most. But sometimes the matured, 'mothering' instinct gets too ripe and becomes a 'smothering' instinct. Pet owners can develop a clinging dependency on their pets. E. B. White, the American writer, said of the Pekinese, an 'infantised' breed, 'Ladies choose'm to clutch to their bosom.'

There are other reasons why people play separation games with their pets. In spite of her rotund appearance, Susie is an attractive little dog. She is a gentle thing, plays lots of games with her owner and is generous with her affection, her only drawback being that before her teeth were removed, being licked by Susie was like being licked by a frog. Unlike many of her Chihuahua compatriots Susie genuinely liked people. That's important because any psychologist will tell you that being liked increases the likelihood that you will like in return. And the psychologist will also tell you that if you happen to be insecure you will be even fonder of the person – or pet – that likes you. Which might be one of the reasons why the acting profession is rife with pets!

Susie is also attractive for other reasons. We are attracted to other people who we feel are honest and loyal and we are attracted to people who have certain skills and abilities or competencies. This attractiveness applies to pets as well. Susie has abilities that Bronwyn Jones finds attractive and the dog exudes the inferred generic canine attributes of loyalty and honesty. Mrs Jones is a very nurturing person and would probably be miserable with a highly independent dog; but Susie isn't independent. Through selective breeding and through her early training Susie has become a dependent dog who enjoys being 'mothered' (or, to be more accurate, 'leadered').

Separation games can be much worse than the game Mrs Jones plays with Susie. Because many pet owners develop a more intense attachment to their pets as the animals get older, the incidence of separation games increases proportionately with the advancing age of the pet. This is in part because, regardless of your enlightenment, regardless of your pragmatism and common sense, the longer you have a pet in your home, the longer you feed it and house it and care for it, although consciously you may say that your dog or cat is one of your possessions and no more than that, subconsciously you think of it as human. The American law courts have recognised this fact and in awarding damages to a woman

And beor of all, you're
so ugly you need me

whose pet poodle was disposed of after its death, not in the
manner requested, the judge said, 'In ruling that a pet such as
a dog is not just a thing, I believe that the plaintiff is entitled
to damages beyond the market value of the dog. A pet is not
an inanimate thing that just receives affection; it also returns
it. [A pet] occupies a special place somewhere in between a
person and a piece of property.' The judge was probably a fan
of the writer Katharine Whitehorn, who said that dogs are
'half way between people and things'.

Separation games can be played in other ways too. Some
guilt games are really separation games. The owner who is
never satisfied with treatment might actually be playing a
separation game. As far as social games are concerned,
however, I don't want to leave them until we look at where
they are played with most finesse, the bedroom.

3. BEDROOM GAMES

PET: 'IT'S MY BED TOO!'

I have to declare an interest here. My dog Liberty sleeps in
her basket in my bedroom. My children are not offered the
same privilege.

It's always been that way. When I married Julia one of the
first things I did (well, almost one of the first) was to move her
dog Honey and the dog's basket from the hallway into the
bedroom. In Toronto, where I spent my teenage years, my
three Yorkshire Terriers had their baskets in a cupboard in
my bedroom. One of these little dogs was a real runt – a
mistake. She was a genetic freak, a Yorkshire Terrier with a
full head of blond hair and blond feathers on her legs, but a
body that was grey and hairless, downy when she was a pup
but dry and freckled when she was older. This dog, Misty,
apologised for living. You could see it in her eyes. She would
wait until the others, her mother and sister, ate before she
went forward to her bowl to eat. She would wait until the

others went through the door into the back garden before she did, and she lived in her cupboard during the day, avoiding contact with people. Late at night, however, when she thought I was asleep, she would creep out of her cupboard, walk over to the end of my bed, jump up on to it, curl up and go to sleep. She slept there until dawn when she would jump off and retreat to her den.

I remember feeling contented when she leapt on to my bed. I would concentrate on not moving because the slightest move had her retreating to the cupboard. I liked it because the strongest feeling I had for that dog was sorrow, not love, and I was happy that my presence could make her feel more content even if that only occurred deep in the night.

Misty was a Yorkshire Terrier and a runt to boot, a five-pound canine wimp. Oscar is a Great Dane, the equivalent in weight of twenty-four Mistys. He also sleeps on his owner's bed and plays 'It's my bed too!', only sleeping with Oscar brings no contentment to his owners. Panic is more like it. Oscar's owners told me of their problem in an embarrassed, apologetic way. 'We have a little problem with Oscar,' the husband said. 'When he was a pup we let him on the bed. Now that he's full grown we want him off but when I tell him to get off he just growls at me. Sometimes he just lies there and growls. If I give him a push from under the covers with my leg he lifts his head and looks at me and growls. There's fire in his eyes when he looks at me that way and quite frankly I am too frightened to persevere.'

Oscar had commandeered that bed because he was allowed to play 'It's my bed' when he was a pup. The games that a pup learns early in life are the longest lasting and the most resistant to change, and Oscar's owners had inadvertently taught him this one. Oscar was a willing learner because it is in the canine temperament to want to share their den with other members of the pack, especially when they are sleeping. I'm not saying they shouldn't but there should be rules to follow, and the most important is the most obvious. The dog

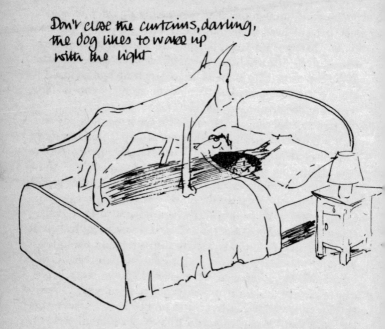

Don't close the curtains, darling,
the dog likes to wake up
with the light

should always be taught that it is the lowest in rank in the pack, that the people who share its den have seniority.

I ask my clients to bear that in mind when they acquire a pup. I tell them that their pup is a pack animal that has slept with its mother and its littermates right up to the day it was bought and moved into his new home, and that it is wrong to isolate that pup in the kitchen or hall or garage on the first night. It is simply too abrupt a change. Pups that are made to live hermits' lives from the start, pups that are isolated for hours on end with nothing to do, are the pups that vent their frustration by whining, yapping, chewing and scratching. Pet owners will tell me how amazed they are that a little pup can completely redecorate a kitchen in a night; tear the newspaper on the floor to shreds, pull the blanket out of the basket and chew it, scratch the wallpaper, mark the doors.

I tell pet owners that when they first bring the pup home it should be allowed to sleep in a bedroom with people and then later, when it is confident in its new surroundings, and more mature, it should be moved to its final sleeping area. This avoids the problems of social isolation but it can also lead to the dog playing games like 'It's my room' or 'It's my bed', so there are certain steps to follow.

Dogs are unlikely to soil around their bedding area but a pup will not have overnight bladder control until it is twelve to sixteen weeks of age and this means that the floor of the room should be covered with newspaper. Make a den for the pup to sleep in. The easiest to make is a cardboard box with a door cut in it. The preparation is as simple as that. Then, putting the pup in its den in your room, go to sleep. The pup will protest. *Do not give in*! Don't coddle it or give it your sweet talk. If you coddle and sweet talk when the pup whines and protests and tries to get on your bed you are teaching it that whining and protesting works! Be firm. I know how hard it is, but be firm. If you let the pup up on your bed now, you may end up with an Oscar who, when you tell him to get off, eyes you as if to say, 'If anyone's leaving— you're leaving!'

I actually followed my own advice with Liberty! She was given a basket in our bedroom but not allowed to sleep on the bed. For better or worse she is, however, allowed to be on the bed when we are not in it. It's the only furniture she is allowed on. She was first trained that when she heard the word 'basket' she was to get off our bed and into hers, and now when I come into the room she just looks at me, raises one eyebrow without lifting her head from her paws and immediately gets off the bed. Other pet owners will prefer that their dog is not allowed on the bed, or does not continue to sleep in the bedroom and this is easy to implement when the dog is housetrained and more mature. Once again, there will be protest when you make the move. A dog that is moved from bedroom to hall or kitchen is bound to protest. If you live in an apartment, invest in a few boxes of chocolates and give them to your neighbours on the day that your dog has to change dens, telling them that the dog might be protesting that night. But again – *don't give in*! You have given your dog the privilege of sharing your den. It is not your dog's right. Dogs have strong wills, however, and as I see it, frequently stronger wills than their owners.

The alternative of having the dog continue to sleep in your bedroom has rewards and advantages. The most obvious reward is the security its presence gives – either real or symbolic security, although the fact that cats and small dogs make great hot water bottles is certainly a plus to many pet owners. Other advantages are even more interesting. When Robert, a Boxer Dog pup, was brought in for his first inoculation, I asked his owner why the dog was named Robert. Dogs usually have their names softened. Robbie is what I expected. Robert is more formal than usual. 'His last

Ten minutes to wake-up time

name is Redford,' she explained and then she paused, looked down, smiled and moved around the end of the examining table closer to me and whispered, 'I sleep with him.'

The disadvantages vary enormously. My only disadvantage with Liberty is that because she is still a pup she wakes up at dawn and a light goes on in her little head that says 'Playtime' and she bounds over to my side of the bed, stands up on the edge with her front feet and drops a tennis ball on to my pillow. I can't deny however that it is a pleasure to wake up to such a smiling face. Other disadvantages are more serious and many of these appear in the bedroom games that people play with their pets.

Owner: 'He'll Be So Lonely If I Leave Him That I Won't Be Able To Sleep'

Dear Mr Blakely,

My wife and I bought a new bed to replace what we had been sleeping on for more than twenty years. We chose a waterbed. Both my wife and I thought that was what a doctor might order for good sleep for an ageing couple – except for one thing. A very important member of our family doesn't like waterbeds and refuses to continue our household habit of sleeping three in a bed. Of course I'm talking about the dog. Because the dog won't sleep on the new bed, my wife has chosen to sleep in the guest room to accommodate the dog's tastes. That leaves me high and dry on my waterbed. Any thoughts?

Signed

Lone Sleeper

Dear Lone Sleeper,

It would seem your wife places the dog in the number one position in your household, and that she feels the dog needs more tender loving care than you do. And she seems to feel she prefers the affection of the dog to yours.

What your wife may not know is that she can have the best of both worlds. If she will return to your new bed it is highly likely the dog will not want to continue to sleep away from his mistress and will arrive back on the bed in due course. If it turns out the dog does not return, your wife may be forced to conclude she loves the dog more than the dog loves her. And that's not the right person-to-pet relationship.

Signed
Tom Blakely

Wise words from Mr Blakely in his *Toronto Star* newspaper column on retirement problems called 'New Adventure'. But I got the feeling that he really wanted to say more only didn't, for fear of telling the whole truth. The whole truth is that the attachment and separation games that are played in the bedroom can sometimes be for real and can sometimes be deadly serious.

I see mrs Hodgkins got cnorody of the cat

I knew a couple like Lone Sleeper and his wife. They were also at retirement age and both doted on their dog. They played 'He'll be so lonely if I leave him' in all situations, not just with their sleeping arrangements. Mitzy went everywhere with her owners. When I first treated her she was already mature. She had the good luck of having owners who cared for her, and genes that programmed her for a long life. Mitzy was a poodle of the old school, one that was born before they became so popular and so inbred, and she proceeded through life with dignity and calm, a serene animal that seemed to say, 'I understand everything' with her eyes.

Her owners took her everywhere. They hadn't been out of the country for close to two decades because they refused to put Mitzy in a kennel for their holiday and, because of quarantine regulations, could not take her abroad and then back again. Not only their holiday revolved around their dog, it seemed to me that their lives did too. They were in to see me at the slightest worry over Mitzy. A scratch at her ear, a cough, an imperceptible limp, anything was enough to justify a visit to the vet. And when they visited they argued. 'If you hadn't taken her for such a long walk she wouldn't have caught a cold.' 'If you pulled the hair out of her ears more frequently like Dr Fogle told you, she wouldn't have so much wax in them now.' They constantly remonstrated with each other over the dog but jointly never ceased to tell me how marvellous she was.

Mitzy of course slept on their bed with them, but as she aged and passed the normal life expectancy of a poodle she inevitably developed progressive old age problems. She didn't develop a heart murmur until she was fifteen, very old for the beginning of that type of problem, but her treatment with drugs to improve her heart's efficiency and to get rid of excess fluid in her lungs was effective, and she ambled on through life in her impressive laid-back way. When she was seventeen, she became incontinent – a greater problem.

At first her incontinence seemed to respond to a diet change. It wasn't an incontinence caused by bladder infection, it was, for lack of a better term, old age incontinence. Later that year I treated her with both female hormones and anabolic hormones. I again was able to improve her condition with the latter, but eventually her night-time incontinence became unremitting. Mitzy's owners didn't mind as much as you would expect. 'She's my best friend,' both of them told me independently, at one time or another while I knew them, and early on, when Mitzy's incontinence first developed, they had 'plasticised' their bed so that Mitzy could continue sleeping with them. So that they could continue sleeping with Mitzy! The end of their bed was covered in a plastic tarpaulin on which bath towels were laid and each morning Mitzy's owners would remove the wet towels, clean her so that she didn't suffer from any urine burns and lay fresh clean towels on the bed.

Mitzy continued to fade but she did so with dignity and continued to enjoy her life and be a good companion. Eventually her multitude of problems became overwhelming. Over the years her heart murmur progressed until her cough was no longer controllable with drugs, her liver was so large that it occupied half of her abdomen, and her ability to take any exercise became minimal. She lost weight and developed signs of kidney failure and I suggested that it was time for the owners to let go, for them to let me put her down.

They wouldn't let go. They couldn't. And Mitzy lost her dignity. It was sad and distressing for me to see a dog that I respected so much reduced to such a state. She finally did die near the end of her eighteenth year and her owners grieved deeply. They both cried their hearts out when they brought her body in to me and consoled each other, holding each other's trembling hands. But Mitzy's owners were divorced a year later. All the time I had known them they had been playing games, ostensibly saying that they couldn't bear to be separated from their dog, couldn't bear to sleep without her, whereas in truth that dog was the only glue holding them together. Their caring for the dog was used to paper over the cracks in their marriage, and when they no longer had a dog to care for, the paper rotted and the marriage fell apart.

Indulging your dog is, of course, not always that harmful. What I am saying is that pet owners who say, 'My dog can't live without me,' are really saying, 'I can't live without my dog,' and that the reasons they can't live without their dogs might be pretty inconsequential or as serious as the problem that Mitzy's owners had. When pet owners say, 'My dog is my best friend,' they might feel that way because of the psychology of pet ownership which I have discussed in chapter one, but equally they might feel that way because they have displaced their dependency on to a dog because there isn't a human around who fills that role.

His jealousy I can stand, her snoring I can't

In practice I see it as a fact – a regrettable but hard fact. The attachment and separation games that pets play are honest, uncomplicated and truthful. They lay their cards on the table. 'I want to be stroked because it makes me feel secure and tells me that you are my leader.' 'I want to sleep in your room with you because I feel more secure when I am with my pack.' 'I'm going to bay at the moon if you leave me because that's how I call my pack and tell them what's cooking.'

The attachment and separation games that we play with our pets are much more complicated. Most people I see have fine relationships with their pets – logical, sensible and pragmatic. The pet is a member of the family and although his or her rights are respected the pet isn't 'used' for any reason other than for the joy of having one. But quite a few urban people do 'use' their pets to satisfy needs that are not being met from more appropriate sources. It would be a value judgement on my part to say it is wrong, because practically speaking these needs probably won't be met from any other sources. It still doesn't make it any less sad.

CHAPTER THREE

Eating Games

1. STARVATION GAMES

PET: 'I CAN'T EAT *THAT*!'

Dogs and cats are dramatically effective at playing eating games. They are so effective because they are so good at training their owners. The dog that is a clever psychologist trains its owner from the very first day it enters its new home. 'You come when called' is the dog's first objective. It knows that if it makes this breakthrough anything goes.

The pet dog goes on to train its owner with these objectives in mind. 'You anticipate my needs.' 'You understand my every desire.' 'You only choose the best.' If the dog successfully meets these training objectives then it is ready to play starvation games knowing with a reasonable certainty that it will win.

Sean O'Casey, a one-year-old Irish Setter, was brought to me because of his poor skin and coat condition and chronic stool problems. His owner had followed Sean's own advice and was feeding him three pounds of fresh meat each day. Sean thought he was on to a good thing, he had trained his owner very well: no hard biscuits or tasteless bread or sticky rice. Life was a dream. Sean simply played 'I can't eat that' whenever he was given anything other than fresh meat, and because most pet owners think that dogs are carnivores, Sean's owner complied with his dog's culinary demands as he had complied with his dog's other demands.

Dogs aren't carnivores. They are omnivores. The staple diet of a Canadian timber wolf is not fillet of Bambi as so many people believe, it's lots of mice – whole mice, that includes what the mice have eaten. Wolves get their minerals and carbohydrates by eating the innards of the animals they kill. Dogs are anatomically built the same as wolves – very large stomachs and relatively short intestines – and feeding on whole mice would be as nutritious for Fou Fou or Duke as it is for their forest cousins. Society, however, would frown upon our feeding our dogs a diet of freshly killed whole rodents or feeding our cats still warm robins and sparrows. We have sanitised our own need for meat by making the killing as remote as possible, and because we treat our pets as family members we want to distance them from reality too, so we feed them 'people' food or dog food dressed up to look like 'people' food.

It wasn't easy to convince Sean to eat dog biscuit and canned dog food. Sean had been allowed as a pup to dictate what he ate and he did it simply by playing 'I can't eat that'. It's a neat trick. Dogs find it easy to manipulate their owners

into believing that they will starve because they can actually go a lot longer without food than we can. Many pet owners genuinely believe that their pets will starve if they don't eat what's offered to them. They see their pets in human terms and forget that dogs are built to gorge themselves on a large meal and then live off it for several days. Eskimo dogs are traditionally fed once every five days yet still have the energy to do intense physical work.

A month later, after Sean's owner had overcome Sean's game and had altered the dog's diet to a can of food, one and a half cans full of biscuit and a vitamin, mineral and unsaturated fatty acid supplement a day, Sean's skin condition and stool formation were normal. Sean's owner calculated that he would be able to buy himself two new small cars during his dog's lifetime from the savings on his food bill!

Dogs love ritual and employ it in their starvation games. Lisson, a six-year-old Standard Poodle, is fed chocolate drops each day but he has been trained to play an enjoyable

I blame the dog-bowl makers myself

and innocuous 'starvation' game. Lisson is given sixteen chocolate drops at a time, once a day. The chocolates are given one at a time and Lisson counts them. If only fourteen or fifteen are given and the owner walks away, Lisson follows and pesters until he gets his full sixteen. He plays an excellent modification of 'I'll starve unless I get what I want', but it's a ritualised modification and I think it's a really good game. His owner sees Lisson's behaviour in simpler terms. 'Crafty bugger,' he says with a twinkle of pride in his eyes.

Starvation games are always intertwined with owner behaviour. If a dog has to fend for itself it will eat almost anything. I remember once while working in the small animal clinic of my veterinary college one summer, I performed a post mortem on a stray dog and found only apple in its stomach. Dogs get away with playing starvation games because they come across owners who let them. Sean's ability to play 'I can't eat that' was based on his owner's lack of understanding of what a dog really can eat. Wimpy plays the same game but is successful because of his owner's insecurities.

Wimpy is a nervous young Yorkshire Terrier who has turned his owner into his servant. Cynthia Belling is a short thin woman with worried eyes that flick awkwardly up to my face then down to the table. She always has a squeezed handkerchief in her hands and carries Wimpy on her right shoulder in a contorted cuddle with the dog's bottom closest to her ear and its body forming a semicircle so that both its head and its tail are facing me. Mrs Belling is usually reluctant to put Wimpy on the examining table and Wimpy is even more reluctant to be put there, so I examine him up on her shoulder, which isn't very difficult because I'm reasonably tall and Mrs Belling is not.

Wimpy has chronic pad problems which probably relate to the terrible diet he got as a pup, and still gets. Because of the people I see in central London, people who are willing to pay for a professional service for their pets, I only see a certain type of pet owner. I see people who are willing to invest in both time and money to ensure the well-being of their pets. It gives me a rose-coloured picture of pet ownership and it also means that I don't see cases of genuine starvation. I do, however, see dogs that are literally starved through kindness, starved through overpampering. Wimpy was starving when I first treated him because he would only eat grilled fillet steak seasoned with salt. He was brought in because of apparent pain and by just looking at the dog and talking to the owner, a diagnosis of calcium deficiency was easy. Mrs Belling couldn't believe that she was actually killing her dog with kindness so I took an X-ray and showed her the thin shadows of what should have been solid straight bones. 'But steak is the only thing he will eat,' she exclaimed in a desperate fashion. 'I've tried everything.'

That was the problem in a nutshell. Wimpy's domestication had become a parody of domestication, and Wimpy was playing 'I can't eat that' because Mrs Belling *wanted* to play 'He won't eat that'.

Owner: 'He Won't Eat That!'

Olivier Pollack has fresh prawns for breakfast. If he doesn't he goes into a sulk. Olivier is a Lhasa Apso. Simon, his owner, is an actor. Olivier's food bill each week is greater than Simon's.

Ten years ago, when Olivier was a pup, he was very ill. He got distemper. He had a fever, vomited, passed blood in diarrhoea and developed double pneumonia. Olivier's nose plugged up daily with a sticky mixture of mucus and pus. His eyes were bloodshot and produced a green yellow discharge. His nose went dry and cracked into long fissures needing lubrication several times daily with a lanolin lotion. Olivier was lucky because the virus didn't affect his nervous system and he didn't develop brain damage or convulsions or even a twitch of the leg, as some dogs do. Through Simon's care and nursing and with the help of drugs and intravenous fluids, Olivier recovered. Only his dry thickened nose and mottled teeth now tell that he endured such a life-threatening illness.

When Olivier was ill, it was important that he eat and drink the most nutritious foods. He was really too ill to want to eat but Simon syringed a concentrated nutrient liquid into the dog's mouth almost hourly for a week. I told Simon to experiment with different foods, especially ones with strong odours, to see if there was anything that might stimulate Olivier to eat on his own. And that's how Olivier discovered prawns.

When it seemed that all was for naught, when it seemed that this nasty and distressing disease would claim another victim, Olivier ate a prawn. We couldn't have been more pleased. Of all the foods that were offered prawns were the most nutritious. Not only was he eating, but he was eating something that would give his body the protein it needed to build up its defences and recover.

At first Olivier had to be hand fed and only ate one prawn but later that day, although he still wouldn't get up, his ears perked up when he was offered more. By the next day Olivier got up and tottered over to his food bowl to eat a few himself. Within a week he was demolishing almost half a pound of prawns a day.

Once he started eating on his own, Olivier's recovery was rapid, but his illness changed the relationship between the owner and his dog. Simon is an actor who lives alone. Olivier, named after Simon's acting idol, Laurence Olivier, is his live-in companion. The relationship would have always been a close one. But Olivier's illness as a pup created a bond between the owner and the pet of greater emotional consequence than Simon knew he was capable of. For almost two weeks, when Olivier was a helpless looking toy of a pup, Simon held that dog on his lap and syringed food into its mouth. He cleaned the discharge from Olivier's eyes and nose. He rubbed lanolin lotion on to the cracked skin. He cleared away the dog's diarrhoea and put ointment on its inflamed anal region. And he gave physical comfort because the pup seemed to want it and Simon felt the need to give it. He talked to the pup. He tried to cheer it up. He put a greater emotional investment in that pup then he had probably ever put in any human. And he got his reward.

Their relationship had started in a normal way – an owner and his dog. But because of Olivier's illness it accelerated within a week, through the stage of simple social contact, to one of social intimacy. The pup's genuine need – life or death need – for Simon stabilised the relationship and gave gratification to both of them. Many people will nurse their pets through trying times because they feel an obligation to do so. But I see too many people like Simon not to know that an equal number thrive on the nursing, relish the caring, and enjoy the comfort *they* get from nursing any animal through a crisis. The reward for Simon was faster and greater than usual because he was able to form a genuine intimate relationship with a living thing.

We are a society that culturally doesn't give a great opportunity for intimacy, certainly in public. For whatever reason, Simon has always lived alone and never mixed in the intense social life of the acting world. Simon isn't the only pet owner to get a social reward from his relationship with his pet. Just routine playing with and attention to your pet gives you the ultimate social rewards of closeness, friendship, understanding and contact. It doesn't under normal circumstances displace relationships with other humans either. And in a sense, interacting with pets is easier and more 'elegant' than interacting with other people, simply because with pets you don't have to beat about the bush. Wasteful moves aren't necessary. The relationship can be neat, clean and uncluttered. To quote Dr Eric Berne, the writer of *Games People Play*, one more time, 'Beautiful friendships are often based on the fact that the players compliment each other with great economy and satisfaction so that there is a maximum yield from a minimum effort from the games they play with each other . . .'

Olivier recovered and when he did I suggested changing his diet back to dog food. I don't know how earnestly Simon tried but Olivier, when given the choice between succulent prawns and canned food and biscuit, made the obvious choice. Simon wasn't going to argue. He just couldn't bear to see the dog not eating again and that's why Simon plays 'He won't eat that'.

A dog's eating habits are formed in puppyhood and are completely dictated by what we permit. If we decide that a can of food and some biscuit, or a packet of soft moist food or a dry 'complete' diet is what it gets, the dog will be content to eat what it is given. But if you give a dog a choice between a shrink-wrapped synthetic hamburger and a piece of raw fillet steak, or between a cheese-flavoured soya protein creation or a buttered grilled cheese sandwich it is foolish to expect the dog to willingly go back to the less tasty food, even if the commercially produced foods are more balanced and nutritious. Dogs will play starvation games because their taste buds aren't dumb and they know what a treat is available if they persevere long enough.

Olivier's story continues. Olivier turned ten this year and I

*A child's high chair! — I've a good mind
to leave the steak*

sent Simon a letter suggesting that it would be a good idea, because of the dog's age, to give him a complete physical examination; a 50,000 mile check-up which includes tests on a fasting blood sample to check out about sixteen body function activities. Olivier seemed in excellent condition but for two facts. His liver was physically enlarged and, although all his other liver function tests were normal, one of them, his serum alkaline phosphatase, was quite high indicating that there was a lot of connective tissue replacement of healthy liver tissue – cirrhosis of the liver. I telephoned Simon and told him. His reply was simple. 'I guess that means he'll have to go without his evening Martini,' he said. My jaw was too slack to reply. I had known that dog for ten years and had treated it for ten years but didn't learn until then that to celebrate the dog's recovery from distemper, Simon had made himself a drink and had offered some to Olivier. The dog liked it and from that day on shared one each evening with his owner.

2. GLUTTONY GAMES

PET: 'FEED ME!'

In the stage play *Little Shop of Horrors* the main character was a carnivorous plant named Audrey that had learned to talk. Its first words were, 'Feed me!' Audrey grew and grew until she finally took up all the room in the florists shop where she lived. When I saw Audrey she reminded me of some of the dogs and cats I see.

Many pet owners firmly believe that feeding a dog is what makes it loyal, but they are wrong. Dogs are not genetically programmed to ask for mothering – to be fed. They are programmed for companionship. They want a leader–follower relationship,. with most dogs willing to be followers. They are loyal because of the companionship we give them, not the food we feed them, but dogs learn to play 'Feed me!' because for many of them there is nothing much else to do.

For lots of dogs, mealtime is the most exciting time of the day. These are the dogs that lead sedentary lives, underactive animals that suffer from stimulus hunger and whose only excitement comes from the satisfaction of wolfing down a meal. Dogs are also astute at learning that begging also gets rewards, usually food rewards. Playing begging games serves two purposes for the dog. First of all it gives it something to do, a way of breaking the monotony of life. And second, the end of the game means a food reward. Dogs are willing to walk on their hind legs, give a paw, or roll over and whistle a few bars from 'Smoke Gets in Your Eyes' because they rapidly learn that these are the strange ways that people like them to say, 'Feed me!'

Dogs and cats are deliciously adept at telling their owners they are hungry. Stanley, a Cocker Spaniel, picks up his food bowl and carries it to his owners when he is hungry, dropping it at their feet. Fritz, a Dachshund, on the other hand, picks up his metal water bowl and bashes it against the fridge until he gets his owner's attention. My favourite technique is employed by a cat who when it is hungry, and this is usually just before dawn, dips his paw in his water bowl then goes over to his owner's bed, jumps up and splashes him in the face. Who says that dogs and cats are incapable of abstract thought!

Get the can-opener, Martha, the dog's juggling again

When dogs and cats do not get their own way, when owners do not respond to their 'Feed me!' games, they steal. Stealing is our term for it. From the animal's perspective they are simply fending for themselves, behaving as normal cats and dogs and 'capturing' their own meal. Sweetpea Allen, a lilac Siamese, corners her prey on the top shelf of the kitchen cupboard. She climbs the open shelves, knocks her prey off the shelf, pounces on it and slashes it with her claws. Sweetpea is obsessed with Ritz crackers and will do anything for them. 'My cat is a thief,' Mr Allen tells me, but in truth Sweetpea is just playing a normal eating game.

My old dog Honey played a similar game in her latter years when I took her to the park. 'Feed me!' is a game that older dogs play with increasing dedication because as they get over the hill, food and feeding can increase in importance. They can become obsessed with food. Honey was never really interested in sex but there were other things in her life that were of extreme importance. Exercise was the most important, and she was passionate for car rides because she knew that more often than not they were associated with play, retrieving thrown tennis balls, a swim in the Serpentine. But as she grew older her desire for exercise dropped. Her interest in other things dropped too and even worn socks eventually held no pleasure for her. She always remained passionate for car rides, however, so much so that sometimes in her waning years I let her stay in my parked estate car all afternoon because I knew she was so contented there and I didn't have the heart to make her leave.

As her interest in some of the more active pastimes of dogs diminished, her obsession with food increased. It started in the park, almost imperceptibly. One day, instead of bringing back the tennis ball I had thrown, she started back then dropped it and walked over to a picnicking family and stared at them, pleadingly. 'Feed me!' She began doing this quite frequently. On one of these occasions, I can't remember exactly when, she was fed and pretty soon she was playing the game with finesse. As the months and years progressed she changed her park pastimes from 'Play with me' to 'Feed me' games. I would take her to the park and she would have a short stroll, do sort of a symbolic somersault and rub her back on the ground, kicking her legs up in the air, then get up, shake herself and set to the serious business of searching for picnickers. People eat in Hyde Park all the year round and sooner or later she would find her prey. 'Feed me,' she would say with an alert yet pleading look in her old grey eyes.

Even in senility most dogs crave food and Honey lived so long that she did develop signs of senility. In her sixteenth year she started to bark for no apparent reason. We would be in the kitchen or bedroom or somewhere and would hear her bark. I'd come downstairs and see her lying on the floor in the living room, staring into the middle of nowhere, and she'd bark again. I never understood Robert Frost's short verse until then.

> The old dog barks backwards without getting up
> I can remember when he was a pup

I took that barking to mean 'Feed me' although I might be wrong. Barney Pertwee is another old Golden Retriever who is a bit past his prime. His owners have told me that Barney

pants when he's forgotten where his water bowl is, a pretty symbolic 'Feed me' manoeuvre. Neither Honey nor Barney can compare with my oldest patient who learned to play a unique 'Feed me' game before I was born. Hendrik, a forty-eight-year-old African grey parrot, blind with cataracts, eats a chicken wing each day. And yes, when his owner comes in from work, the parrot says, 'Hello.' Then he says, 'Feed me.'

I knew that Honey's life had to come to an end when she stopped playing the 'Feed me' game. One morning it was just too obvious that she was even loosing interest in her obsessive quest for food. It was how we knew it was time to close a very important chapter in my family's life. When an old dog is no longer obsessed with food it is no longer interested in living.

OWNER: 'BUT I ONLY FEED HIM ONCE A DAY'

Willy Hughes is a Springer Spaniel. I think. His pedigree says he's a Springer Spaniel but he looks like the Goodyear blimp. Actually he looks worse. His back is square. His eyes bulge from their sockets and he's slung so low he constantly catches his prepuce on the ground and injures himself. There is no way he can clean himself up after he eliminates and this means that he almost always has dried feces caked in the hair around his tail. Willy doesn't lift his leg when he urinates. That's too much of an effort at his size so he just stands when he pees and shoots himself in the belly. Willy doesn't smell too nice either. The dog is grotesque. He looks ugly, yet whenever I raise the question of his weight I always get the same answer. 'But I only feed him once a day.'

I don't know why. I can't explain it. Whenever I raise the subject of a dog's weight with his owner, the owner always has the same reply. 'But I only feed him once a day.' The fact that they are feeding 2500 calories to a dog that needs perhaps 800 calories doesn't enter the picture. Frequency of feeding, not quantity, is the inevitable point that owners want to discuss.

Sometimes there are medical reasons for a dog's gluttony and sometimes there are metabolic ones. Tufty, a Dachshund with an overactive adrenal gland, is a food obsessive because he can't help it. His owners say that they wish that in his next life he returns as a gannet and fulfils his apparent life purpose. In many gluttony games, however, overstuffing is owner-mediated. Pets get overstuffed for the owner's own psychological reasons.

In its simplest form, overstuffed people keep overstuffed dogs, and when I am confronted with a fat dog and a fat owner who says, 'But I only feed him once a day,' I know I'm up against a brick wall and I barely even try to overcome the problem. Other veterinary surgeons are far more ambitious and hold a sort of 'fat dogs anonymous' meeting where the owners of fat dogs sit around a table and discuss what they do and how they can improve on their present feeding habits. Many owners of fat dogs, however, are not fat themselves and they are feeding their dogs because they feel an irresistible need to do so.

Obsessive feeders feed their dogs excessively in part because of the signals they receive from their pets. Cats use body language. They headbutt and writhe around your legs. Dogs paw you or, if they are small enough, lick or try to get on your lap. Even non-mammals are good at signalling to us. My African grey parrot, Humphrette, a parrot that meows like a Siamese because she spends each day in reception, bends her head for a tickle whenever I am near her, and once she feels my fingers, presses into them with all of her body. If a human were sending these signals to another human, the interpretation would be unequivocal affection or love or admiration.

Pets offer more. A dog never assaults you with words that might alter your opinion of him. He's natural and honest. He only puts his foot in his mouth to chew his nails. Because pets offer some people so much, those people want to offer as much as they can in return and in many cases what they erroneously

she's like me
- large boned

offer is food. It is erroneous because if they really want to reward their pets for their loyalty and dedication they should be giving them more exercise.

Food rewards come in many ways. Many Iranians in London add garlic, onions and peppers to their cat's food so that 'my cat enjoys her food more'. Phil Drabble on television absently shares his sandwich with his dog while he speaks to the camera, and I'm sure that mine is not the only family that has, on occasion, bought an extra McDonalds for the dog. A point is reached when these rewards become excessive and are no longer in the dog's interest, and that is what happened with Willy. Willy is also caught in a vicious circle because the fatter he gets the less exercise he takes and the less exercise he takes the fewer calories he needs. Dogs like Willy can lose weight if their owners let them. I've discovered through experience that the best way to reduce the weight of a pet whose owner plays 'But I only feed him once a day' is to get that dog away from the owner for a few weeks. Because of the dependency that owners so very often have on their fat dogs, this can be difficult, and I sometimes wait for six to nine months until the owners go away before taking a pet in and putting it on a reduced calorie and increased exercise regimen. Owners can scarcely believe they are picking up the same pet when they return, and almost invariably they control its weight after that because they genuinely do want to do what's right for their pet only they didn't have the heart to 'starve' it back to normality.

Pet owners are happy for their pets to eat anything that is nutritious and good for them, except for one thing, and that is why pets and their owners practise a very special type of eating game.

3. FECES GAMES

PET: 'IT'S MY DESSERT'

She came out of the bushes with it in her mouth. Libby was twelve weeks old. She had just had her meal and I had taken her into the private gardens we have access to for her to attend to her bodily functions. It was as if she had just discovered Disneyland. Now she was enjoying the most pleasing game of all, for she had found a fecal bolus like no other. It was like a gorilla's turd, the Jolly Green Giant's dropping. It stuck round and firm out of both corners of her mouth and her eyes twinkled as she pranced in front of me and said with pride, 'Look what I found – all by myself. It's my dessert.'

I got annoyed and said, 'Drop it!', forgetting that I hadn't got that far in her training and was only at the stage where I could command her to sit and then, saying 'Drop it!', take something from her mouth. She disobeyed and pretended she was a Lipizzaner horse trotting with her head erect and her tail held high in the air, all the time mouthing the goody in her jaws, rolling it, repositioning it, chewing on it to get a better grasp. I started to chase her but quickly realised that that was what she wanted me to do, so I stopped, eyed her with a look of fire and bellowed, 'Libby! Sit!' at the top of my lungs. I'm sure that in my anger and preoccupation with what she was doing I said, 'Libby! Shit!' but in either case she stopped her dance and her bum hit the grass, her tail still wagging fiercely and maliciously and her jaws still working on her treasure.

God, I hate these ownership disputes

I walked over to her slowly, glaring at her with a laser look, pointing with my finger as I advanced saying, 'Stay! . . . Stay! . . .' repetitively like a bad record. Her eyes remained filled with glee and she repositioned the mighty turd so that it sat cigar-like in her mouth, bulbous like an overwrapped Havana. I got closer and realised that it wasn't a gorilla's, it wasn't even the Jolly Green Giant's, it was human excrement. I reached Libby and bent down saying, 'Drop!' Her tail wagged faster like an overwound mechanical stuffed toy and in a flash she bolted her treat down. One chew and it was gone. Half a pound of human excrement down her throat. I could have booted her over the fence but restricted myself to saying, 'Bad dog,' slapping her on the snout, and then walking away ignoring her. She followed me imploring, but I wouldn't look at her. After a few minutes I put her lead back on and frog-marched her home.

I controlled myself (with difficulty) because I knew that to a young dog, feces is really dessert. Dogs, like most other members of the canine family, are scavengers and eating feces is not an unnatural act. It is unacceptable from our point of view, however, and is a behaviour that as pet owners we want to eliminate, just as we want to eliminate other normal but unacceptable canine habits such as urine-marking the territory.

Libby's ability and desire to eat excrement is natural. It is in fact part of her built-in survival instinct. When we first went to the kennels where Liberty was born, to see her parents and to choose from their litter, her mother was busy licking up the urine and eating the feces passed by her pups. Just as she had eaten the afterbirths when the pups were born, she was still tidying up after them, removing signs of their presence to protect them from predators. There is an advantage to the mother, too, because feces contains enzymes and minerals and other nutrients which can actually be beneficial. Cattle, for example, are sometimes fed chicken droppings as a food because it is so rich in urea – in theory up to ten per cent of a cow's daily diet could consist of chicken droppings.

Eating feces or *coprophagia*, as the medical term would call it, can persist as a habit as the dog matures. It is also how a dog can pick up roundworms from another dog, for if a dog finds another dog's stool that has been lying on the ground for a sufficient time for the roundworm eggs to change to infectious roundworm larvae, eating that stool will result in a round-worm infestation. Libby's *coprophagia* diversified while she was a pup. She was most interested in eating her own droppings, then other dogs', and finally at the bottom of the list, horses' manure. She was broken of the habit by being walked in the park and gardens after her meals only on a leash and by being given a firm 'No!' and a yank whenever I thought she was going to do any more than take a divine sniff of the stuff. She didn't completely stop playing 'It's my dessert' until she was six months old.

Dogs will eat feces because it is, like anything else that is enjoyable, habit forming, but they also do it for a genuine need. Veterinary surgeons frequently see dogs that eat strange things. Owners will bring their pets in because they lick concrete, eat pebbles or wolf down any dog dropping they can find. The medical term for a depraved appetite such as this is 'pica', and there are sound biological reasons why some dogs eat feces. They probably suffer from an enzyme deficiency, perhaps coupled with a mineral deficiency, and are supplementing their diet the best and most natural way they know how. Courgettes, pumpkin, pineapple and papaya are vegetables and fruits that provide good natural enzyme supplements, and if your dog plays feces games you should make sure it is just a habit, not really a dietary deficiency, before you try to correct it.

Owner: 'How Can My Dog Do Such a Thing?'

My wife got genuinely upset when she saw that Libby was eating, and her distress was similar to the distress many owners feel when they see their pets doing what to us are odious activities.

First of all Julia blamed herself. She hadn't raised her dog well. 'How can my dog do that?' she would say. Then she got angry at her vet. 'There is something seriously wrong with that dog,' she exploded, willing me, imploring me to find a medical answer to justify the dog's behaviour. Our son Ben felt the same way and it's only natural in our society to do so. We see dogs in human terms. Ben looked at Libby's mother lapping up the urine and eating the droppings of her six-week-old pups and he was revulsed. He quite naturally backed away when the bitch came over to him for some tickles. After all he himself had been a helpless infant once yet his mother hadn't . . . , went through his mind. It was unnatural.

I find it strange that in practice my clients are frequently more at ease talking about little Rover taking a cushion off into the corner of the living room and humping it than they are describing to me the quality and texture of Rover's droppings. The very subject of feces clashes with our perceptions on the quality of life. Of course we can always go back to Sigmund Freud for a comment on a matter like this. He said that our discomfort about feces was due to 'an unresolved ambivalence in the human attitude toward anality' and that this was 'incompatible with our aesthetic ideas'.

If a pet owner says to himself, 'How can my dog do such a thing,' I try to remind him of how children feel about their feces and say that dogs have a life-long child-like attitude towards droppings. First of all the droppings are theirs. When a dog passes a stool, it frequently has a sniff before leaving it because as a final gesture it squeezes a little anal gland juice on it and it wants to smell that it is his. Dogs use their feces to mark out territories, they don't look on the stuff as residue or waste the way we do. When a dog goes sniffing feces, he sniffs and says, 'That's mine,' or 'That's Rover's,' or 'That's that dishy little bitch's from down the street.' Feces is property.

In a psychological sense feces is many other things although some of these are harder to grasp because they are symbolic. When Libby was a pup she would carry her feces over to me as if it were a gift. It was an act of patronage; her way of saying, 'You are my leader,' or as most pet owners would interpret it if it were any other object, 'I love you.' We certainly lavish praise on our pets after they have eliminated in the gutter or on the grass and by doing so we are rewarding the dog – giving it love for what it has done – 'stroking' it.

The pup in turn can't help but react positively to its stool because, aside from innate curiosity over its own creation, we reinforce a positive attitude by praising every turd that is passed. That's one of the reasons why feces is so much fun for

It's for you George — another special delivery for the leader of the pack

the dog. Liberty liked nothing more than to have a good play with a pile of her own dung. She relished it! This is also how dogs learn to play elimination games. 'As long as they treat me right, I'll deliver the goods on time and I won't eat them, but if they treat me mean, if they leave me here alone all day, just watch me!'

If pet owners understand all of these things it is then easier for them to cope with their dog's behaviour. I have tried to remind some pet owners who are also parents of how children treat their excrement – finger painting on the walls and all of that – but they are just as revulsed when their children play feces games as when their pets do. There are certain taboo subjects with many people and feces is one of them, although I never know what the others might be. When a cat owner recently asked me why her cat had a discharge from its eyes and was sneezing I told her it was a virus infection. When she asked what type and I told her it was probably a feline herpes virus, she retorted with hurt, '*My* cat doesn't lead *that* type of life,' and marched out of the clinic without waiting for any treatment (or paying her bill). There are dangerous emotional territories for some pets, and dogs that play feces games should proceed with great caution. So should their veterinary surgeons.

CHAPTER FOUR

War Games

1. SEX GAMES

PET: 'HELLO STRANGER (NUDGE NUDGE WINK WINK)'

Surgery was completed by suppertime and Kelly became the first (and only) dog I have known that had to be opened up both front and back at the same time. His problems started innocently enough. Kelly is an eight-year-old male Dandie Dinmont, a salacious little dog with a leering aspect to his nature and a personality profile that would put sex at the top of the list of his preoccupations. Kelly lives on a housing estate north of my practice and has regrettably been given free licence to roam. The result has been that there are quite a few dogs on that estate with strangely short legs and large faces. Kelly is quite experienced at the mating game.

His problem, as I mentioned, started innocently when a new dog – a delectable morsel in his eyes – moved into a nearby house. The newcomer, a West Highland Terrier, was just a pup and her owners fenced in their small back garden so that she could not get out, and other dogs could not get in. The Westie matured and with time started her first season, her first oestrus cycle. Experienced old Kelly was at hand. No fool he, Kelly knew what was happening and he tried to introduce himself to the Westie. It was to no avail. The fencing was Kelly-proof. Disturbed and agitated and undoubtedly frustrated, Kelly took up residence outside the Westie's home. He urinated on everything and he howled plaintively. The Westie may well have been interested in his love calls but her owners were not and they asked politely, I am told, for Kelly's owners to keep him under control. The owners were embarrassed enough to do so and Kelly was kept at home – locked in jail.

Dogs have an exquisitely sensitive sense of smell and Kelly's was better than many. Locking him indoors kept him physically away from the Westie but it didn't keep him from thinking about her. He was restless and irritable and he went off his food; whenever either of his owners took him for a walk he pulled on his lead in a vain attempt to get to his lady.

On the day in question Kelly was left at home alone all morning while both his owners were out. And that was the morning that Kelly created medical history for me because he just flipped out. He'd had it. He'd suffered long enough and in desperation he started eating everything. He scratched at the door and chewed on the wood. He scratched at the carpet and pulled it from the floor. He scratched at the foam rubber

underlay and lifted that too. Then he ate it all. When he was
finished he dragged a cushion off the sofa and sexually abused
it. His owners could tell because of the spots he left on it. And
then it started to hurt.

His owners returned and found him in agony on the floor,
lying in puddles of his own vomit and urine. When he was
brought in to me he had no pain reflex in either hind leg but
was in obvious pain and had a bloated stomach.

X-rays showed that the cause of his paralysis was a slipped
disc and that he had a stomach full of debris. And so in one
day he was opened up on one side – his belly – to empty out
his stomach and tack it back into the right position, and then
flipped over and opened up on the other side – his back – to
remove the offending slipped disc, and its neighbours, to try
and eliminate the paralysis. I suggested castrating him at the
same time but his owners wouldn't even contemplate it.

Kelly's 'stranger' as in 'Hello stranger (nudge, nudge, wink,
wink)' was a cushion, but I imagine there are few people
around who haven't been propositioned by a dog at one time
or another. Male dogs are straightforward. Jilly Cooper says
that most people who have dogs are proud of the fact that
their dogs never forget faces. She says that her dog never
forgot a crutch. Owners of big dogs get really embarrassed
when they bring them in for me to examine and the first thing
the dog does is examine me. You can change your underwear
every ten minutes if you like but dogs will still greet you in the
same canine way – nose between your legs.

Smaller dogs seem to be able to forego the formalities and
are content to clasp on to any available leg or arm; although
there is a breed disposition to behaviour too. Terriers can be
dying but can still summon the energy and the will to ravage
anything. I once castrated a Jack Russell Terrier because he
lived with three entire females and life was a misery to him,
but his owners were back two months later claiming I had
deceived them, showing me the litter of newborn pups to
prove it. I had castrated the dog at noon, yet that evening he

felt well enough (or obsessed enough) to mate with one of his female housemates that was in season and, although his sperm-producing apparatus had been removed that morning, he still had enough swimming around in the ducts to father a litter. I couldn't help but feel proud of him.

Female dogs are less overtly crude in their propositioning. Guests who come to dinner might find large females backing up towards them and if the dog is stroked she cocks her tail to the side revealing the important bits. Little dogs, on the other hand, might actually latch on to arms or legs the way male dogs do, which can be very disconcerting to the owners. 'I don't want to have a gay dog,' I'm told more often than I can remember, and I have to constantly remind pet owners that a bisexual nature is normal in many species, given the social environments we create for them. Look at any herd of heifers or dairy cattle to see what I mean. Cats are even more interesting, but when a male cat says 'Hello stranger,' you'd better get out the chainmail. Sex in catdom is downright nasty.

Flash was dumped on the table and his owner said in an exasperated way, 'He's suddenly attacking me for no reason.' And he was. Flash would lay in wait for his owner–victim. He would stalk her from behind the furniture and then he would pounce, biting her neck. He was carrying out a sex attack.

Flash hadn't always been like that. For years he had been an affectionate pet. He was neutered when he was young and had always lived with the same female owner. To suddenly start attacking was unexpected of him and depressing for his mistress, and it took several months before we knew why. Flash's owner had married and, as social mores have flipflopped during the last two decades, went *off* the birth control pill at that time. She had been taking the pill the entire time she had owned Flash, thereby suppressing her normal ovulation and the hormonal and pheromonal peaks that go with it. Now that she was married she planned to have babies, and Flash experienced a human oestrus cycle in its full maturity for the first time and he liked it. It took a few months before Flash's owner realised that Flash was only attacking her just before her period. He was like a biological indicator – she could anticipate her period from the look in her cat's eyes. We knew that Flash's propositioning was sex hormone related because his mistress's marriage regrettably failed and she went back on to the birth control pill. His attacks stopped almost as suddenly as they had begun.

Like female dogs, female cats aren't as outgoing in their sexual propositioning as their male counterparts but they are much more flamboyant. Veterinary surgeons and their nurses get propositioned all the time, especially from Christmas until June, the best time of year for feline proposing. 'My cat's broken both her hind legs and is screaming in pain,' the telephone caller will tell me in a near panic, not knowing that female cats are weird and wonderful in the ways they tell us they are ready to be mated. And all that affectionate leg rubbing that sometimes goes on isn't just because she's itchy. When cats play 'Hello stranger' they are at least capable

of fulfilling their preordained responsibilities fairly successfully. All that caterwauling usually does mean that something
is happening and, in fact, a female might be mated by several
toms in one night with the toms ritually staring each other
down or actually fighting to determine the sequence of service.
Dogs aren't quite so smart. The dog that has generalised his
mating instinct or the first timer can with single-minded
dedicated purpose leap five-foot fences, cross busy highways,
ford streams, traverse housing estates and overcome countless
other odds to finally find his bitch and mount her from the
wrong end.

Bitches that have finished their season may play a distant
but related version of 'Hello stranger' for the following two
months. When Samantha Collins brought her German
Shepherd bitch Sally to see me I noticed that the owner was
wearing two different shoes. Sally had been very itchy recently
and was waking her owner up at night with her constant
scratching. Sally also looked like a sow, with pendulous teats
and copious milk production. She was having a normal but
exaggerated false pregnancy, which also accounted for why
her mistress had two different shoes on. When Sally has a false
pregnancy she develops a shoe fetish and impulsively collects
shoes, hiding them in her den under the bed. She's a full-
grown German Shepherd and getting under that bed involves
a contortion act in which she pretends she's a turtle, but it also
means that she has an enclosed and easy area to defend.
Although Sally is a gentle Shepherd, she aggressively defends
her litter of shoes, even from her mistress, by growling and
raising her lip to show her canines and incisors. Samantha
Collins has learned how to cope with this game. She moves
her bed as far as she can so that she can reach the littermate
she wants, then says, 'Oh Sally! What a pretty puppy. Nice
Sally. Can I see the puppy?' and sweet talks and charms the
frustrated mother until she is able to touch the shoe she wants.
Still stroking the shoe and talking to it she takes it away and
puts it on. Sally watches incredulously, but she doesn't bite

and lets her owner get away with it. Baby talk is the only way
her owner can get her shoes back from the possessive mother,
but on the morning she brought Sally in to see me she just
didn't have time to go through the whole ritual. Sally needs to
nurture. It's a hormonal imperative, but because of the way
she lives all she has to compensate for her lack of a real litter
are smelly shoes.

OWNER: 'RAPE!'

Pets have fewer hang-ups about sex than people do. With
notable exceptions, they are certainly less obsessed with the
subject.

'Help! My cat's being raped!' Maxine, on reception duty,
didn't know whether it was one of my friends playing a little
game or whether it was for real, so she replied in a way that

would satisfy both possibilities. 'Tell me exactly what's happening.'

'He's out there right now. He's dirty and horrible and he's attacked her from behind. My cat cried out for help but I can't reach her. Oh please help!' There was a plaintiveness in her voice, a despair that sounded only too real, and Max decided that the call was genuine. 'Has your cat tried to escape from him?' she asked. 'She couldn't. He was too fast. She cried out for help but now she's in shock and she can't move. She's just sitting there. Helpless!'

Maxine soothingly explained to the owner that if her cat were not in season the male wouldn't be interested in her and, more important, her cat wouldn't allow the male to mate. 'Sex is different in cats,' she went on. 'It's much more aggressive and vocal than in other animals. The tomcat will bite your cat's neck when he mates and his penis is barbed, not smooth. That's why your cat cried out. She wasn't trying to escape. She was just acting in the natural way cats do when they are mated.'

'That's disgusting!' said the caller and hung up. It became my nurses' favourite story for weeks.

People reveal much about themselves through their relationships with their pets and the area of sex particularly can be a flashpoint of emotion. Spend some time in any veterinary surgeon's reception room and sooner or later you will meet 'the flasher'. 'The flasher' is usually a large dog and usually short-haired. Weimaraners and Dobermanns make good flashers. The flasher will sit in reception, usually grinning and panting, flashing at anything and anybody who passes. Pat him on his head and he smiles and flashes. Just say 'Hello' to him and he does the same. Reception room flashers are happy dogs and usually cause no harm. But watch the reactions they bring. Some people will comment on the flasher's proclivity but others will virtually shield their dogs' eyes from the offending appendage. 'Don't look, Dorothy, he's just a dirty old man.'

Put it away, Bruno,
mrs Simpkin isn't impressed

These people probably find sex unnatural themselves and
forget that domestication hasn't really greatly changed basic
animal behaviour, it has just made it easier to observe. Joe
Brown, the singer and recorder producer, tells the story of
singing at the Palladium in London one year and deciding
that this time, to be a little different, he would sing a love song
to his dog. He owned an amenable young Labrador and when
the time came to sing this song he knew he could rely on his
dog to sit quietly and attentively while he crooned sweet
nothings to it. Joe Brown sang his song to the audience and his
dog obediently performed his duties with the discipline of any
good well-trained Labrador, but Brown couldn't understand
why, as he sang his way through the gentle love song, the
audience started to snicker. The snickering began in the first

rows and then like a gentle wave breaking on the beach it built to a crescendo flowing through the stalls of the theatre until the sound of laughter overwhelmed his guitar and his voice. He continued singing because he's a professional and only noticed the wicked grin on his dog's face, and the cause of the mirth, after he had finished the number.

Neutering pets is a social necessity in large urban areas if we are to maintain population control of dogs and cats and if we are to make their lives more content. Dense concentrations of dogs such as occur in cities like London are socially unnatural. They would never exist in more natural surroundings. Sweden's attitude, where it is now illegal to neuter male or female dogs unless there are medical considerations, is all wrong. All it has done is dramatically increase the frequency of emergency hysterectomies because of uterus infections, a far riskier surgical procedure than an elective operation.

We have wisely avoided problems like the ones the Swedes have created for themselves, but the increased neutering of pets in Britain and North America, combined with changing sexual mores in human society, has brought a few new problems for the veterinary surgeon.

'She wants a vasectomy for her cat,' my receptionist said. 'I've talked to her about it but she wants to speak to you.' My cue. A nurse at the end of her tether.

The caller was a young New Yorker, a Brooklynite transplanted to London. Practising in the middle of London means that I see a cosmopolitan array of clients: Arab oil millionaires, Filipino housekeepers, Japanese businessmen, Polish housepainters, Australian fashion designers, South American exiles, Nigerian generals, South African emigrants, Pakistani retailers, Israeli draft dodgers, but mostly quasi-permanent American expatriates. The settled American population in central London is the same as that of a good-sized town in the United States. Diplomats and military families are in a minority, outnumbered by American families assigned by their businesses and affluent anglophile Americans

Wild? I'm positively FERAL

who can afford to keep a permanent home in London. Americans make up a goodly percentage of my clients and, as a rule, try to become more English than the English. They remember their formal training in manners and shake hands profusely. They speak very quietly and all buy Burberrys as soon as they get off their planes. They're a treat. But Brooklyn isn't America.

'Why am I speaking to you?' she said. 'All I want is an appointment for a vasectomy for my cat.' I asked her if she knew what a vasectomy was. 'He'll still smell like a tomcat and he might spray your walls too,' I said. 'The only thing a vasectomy will do is make sure that he doesn't father any kittens – nothing more. It won't improve any of the other problems you might be having with him.'

'I don't have any problems. My cat doesn't have any problems! All I wanna do is make sure he doesn't make some pussy pregnant, that's all. Lissen! I don't know why I'm telling you this, but I love my cat. And he loves me. He's never going to look at me one day like some shmuck and say "Beverly, it's been nice knowing ya. We've had a good thing going but so long." He loves me and I'm not going to take away his balls. I want him to still be able to –' and I learned how to perform a vasectomy.

Owners' attitudes to sex are not always that protective. Most pet owners are freely willing to discuss ovariohysterectomies on females and to have them carried out. But watch out when castration of male dogs is discussed. Wives invariably say, 'I'll have to ask my husband' – something they seldom do when it comes to decision-making on neutering a female. A woman will frequently reply, 'My husband doesn't want it done,' and flatly refuse to discuss the subject. On the

Ok, so long as he can still have meaningful relationships afterwards

occasions when a wife brings her husband in for a joint discussion with me about neutering their dog, I only have to use the word 'castration' to make the husband sit up in the chair, cross his legs and pay attention. Wives say that if they have their delinquent male dogs castrated without their husband's approval, then their husbands will consciously or unconsciously feel that they are *really* trying to castrate *them*. Who knows? Maybe they are. When a wayward Westie latched on to my leg one day while I was sitting talking to his female owner, she looked at me and said, 'I'll tell you a secret. Living with that dog has made me understand my husband an awful lot better.'

Sex games are interesting and usually harmless but an integral part of War Games. There is a point where they blend with associated aggression games and this is where they become harmful.

2. AGGRESSION GAMES

PET: 'I HATE . . . UMBRELLAS . . . NEWSPAPERS . . . STRANGE NOISES . . . VISITORS . . . SUITCASES . . . *You*!'

'It's like living with Margaret Thatcher,' he said, dumping his old-fashioned fifteen-pound Yorkshire Terrier on the table. 'We can't make a move without a stern reprimand. She thinks she's always right and we should never interfere with her decisions.'

That morning, Scruffy had attacked Jim Wallace again as he read the morning newspaper. It wasn't the first time that she had acted aggressively with her owner. She always got upset when Mr Wallace read the paper and in fact went slightly berserk each time the paper was delivered. Given a chance and a copy of *The Times*, Scruffy was more efficient at destruction than the latest electronic shredding machine.

At other times Scruffy was a soft apologetic Yorkie. She seemed to enter nirvana when her belly was rubbed. But newspapers made her mean and aggressive and when she was mean and aggressive she didn't care who she bit.

Scruffy's aggression is a fear aggression that she acquired when she was a pup, but there are many other types of aggression games that pets play. Leadership aggression games, in which the dominant member of the pack (or household) maintains his decision-making capacity through aggressive displays, will be covered in the next chapter under 'Dominance Games'. Territorial protection games will follow at the end of this chapter under Territory Games.

Certain breeds have a built-in propensity for aggression. Their aggression games are genetic in origin. My nurses recently asked me to perform a post-mortem on a Persian cat. I was surprised at how heavy the bag was, and when I split it open on the post-mortem table all I saw was earth. The cat was completely covered in matted rolled balls of earth embedded throughout its coat. There was so much earth that I couldn't differentiate one end from the other. I had never seen anything like it.

Once I examined the body more closely I found its head and saw that one eye was punctured and deflated and there was blood mixed with the earth in its mouth. By separating the hair over its body I found multiple puncture wounds to the chest and abdomen and a larger tear near the bladder through which a loop of intestine was protruding. I telephoned the owner and explained the findings, that the cat had been torn to death by another animal – probably a large dog – and I asked her about the earth on its body. She told me that she had seen a freshly dug pile of earth in her back garden, like a mole hill, and went to investigate. One foot down she found her cat. Her eight-year-old Rottweiler bitch, a dog that had lived with this cat for years, had inexplicably killed and buried it. The Rottweiler's aggression was genetic, similar to the aggression that is bred for in other breeds, the extreme example being the American Pit Bull Terrier, a dog bred for only one true purpose – to fight with and kill other dogs as 'sport'. It is in its own way a predictable aggression but extremely serious in circumstances such as this where, aside from the dead cat, the owner had four small children.

Nervous aggression can be genetic although it can also be a learned form of aggression which is easily reinforced. Nervous aggression is what many German Shepherds and Dachshunds suffer from. These dogs are called *angstbeisers* in German, or 'nervous biters', and I can't think of a comparable term in English that so well describes them. Our problem is that because of the games we play with them, we are constantly reinforcing their nervous aggression. The *angstbeiser* doesn't really *want* to bite people and if given the opportunity will go out of its way to avoid confrontations. *Angstbeisers* hide from visitors. They hide from their veterinary surgeons too, cowering behind their owners, not because I have ever done anything to cause pain or distress (there are many dumb dogs I have done horrible things to that bound back in like morons, only remembering the vitamin tablet bribe they have previously been given) but because I am strange or unfamiliar – not a member of the pack. Owners of little *angstbeisers* reinforce the aggressive games their pets play through the ways they cope with their pets' aggression. Nervous Yorkshire Terriers, for example, are frequently picked up and cuddled when they bark nervously at strangers, but all that this does is tell the dog that if it barks and shows signs of nervous aggression it will be rewarded with cuddles and soothing words. The owner is reinforcing the game.

Barbara Woodhouse says that there are 'no bad dogs' and although her sentiment is correct she is wrong in fact. Every veterinary surgeon will tell you about his psychopath patients, his canine terrorists, his Rambos, who from the day they are born prepare for war. It's true that pet owners can produce maladjusted canine delinquents by over-indulging their dogs when they are young or by not dominating them sufficiently. But it is equally true that there are some dogs that are just born to be emotional misfits and regardless of the training

Let's put it this way, no one calls me a psychopath – and lives!

they receive grow up to become fully-fledged bloodthirsty hooligans. Their aggression is psychopathic. A classmate of my son's was recently followed home from school by a German Shepherd. The dog tracked him and when the boy got to his front door it attacked. The attack was unpredictable and inexplicable. There had been no provocation, not even an 'escape' attempt by the boy, who was well experienced with dogs, that could have induced a 'chase the quarry' response. Both the boy and his mother, who intervened, required hospital treatment for their injuries.

It doesn't matter what canine reform school you send these dogs to, they will always be psychopaths. I described one of these dogs in *Pets and Their People*, a dog I knew was a problem from the first time I saw him as a ten-week-old pup, and which was eventually destroyed only after it tore the scalp off the owner's four-year-old son. These dogs are true misfits and because their bizarre aggression might be genetic they should not be used for breeding. If they are large dogs with the potential to cause serious harm, they should be destroyed.

Scruffy Wallace, the Yorkshire Terrier that attacks newspapers, plays a fairly innocuous game in comparison. Scruffy plays 'I hate newspapers', a game which has as many variations as there are dogs. My dog started to develop a game called 'I hate umbrellas' until I put a stop to it. 'I hate visitors' is one of the most common variations and one of the most serious. 'I hate blacks' is self-evidently one of the most embarrassing and 'I hate *you*' is the most upsetting to the owner, but the advantage is that of all the aggression games, the fear-induced aggression games 'I hate . . .' are those most amenable to change. Because they are so common and so important I will explain how these games can be overcome, using Scruffy as an example.

In the old housetraining pamphlet I used to hand out I wrote, 'Pups will only understand the reason for discipline if they are disciplined while they are messing in the wrong place or within a few seconds of their finishing. Use your sternest sergeant's voice and scold the pup. Never hit it with your hand because that might make it hand shy. Use a rolled up newspaper and give it a thump on its backside, not to hurt it, just to let it know you mean business. You only need to do this once or twice. After that a threat with a newspaper should work a treat.'

It was pretty embarrassing when I realised that I was the reason that Scruffy hates newspapers. When I wrote that pamphlet I didn't know enough about simple canine behaviour. I hadn't received any formal training on the subject at university and didn't know that fear induction was at its most critical when a pup is between eight and twelve weeks of age; that this is the time we have to be most careful with what we do with our pup. Scruffy's housetraining began during that time and newspapers became that dog's mortal enemies. Newspapers are what abused her when she was a pup and once she grew up, tough terrier that she was, she let them and anybody associated with them know that she would take no more.

If I had made different housetraining recommendations for Scruffy, she wouldn't have learned to play 'I hate newspapers'. When we got Liberty I practised the Mark Two version of housetraining and it worked. She was simultaneously trained to void herself indoors on newspaper and outdoors both in the gutter and on the lawn. We instituted a reward scheme. When she emptied herself in the gutter in the mews behind our hours, or on the lawn, or on newspaper, she was given lavish praise. (Thank you for your gift!) Sometimes she was also given a yeast-flavoured vitamin tablet as a food reward. The behaviourist calls a food reward a 'positive reinforcer'.

Inside the house she had her reward system but there was also discipline for misbehaviour. We started by covering the floor with newspaper and restricting her to two rooms and the hall. Pups will usually want to urinate after they wake up, or after play or after food, so we watched her carefully at those times. When she used a newspaper she was praised. Libby caught on within a week and we were able to reduce the printed mayhem in the house to an *Observer* in the kitchen, the *Standard* in the hall and *The Times* in the living room, but this left 'room' for mistakes.

All the kids were programmed on what to do if they saw Libby peeing on the carpet. They were told to be dramatic, to time themselves well and to use an element of surprise. When she urinated on the paper she was to be praised. But if she didn't, first of all a stern 'Bad dog!' was to be said as she was urinating. The tone of voice is important. Barbara Woodhouse is such a successful trainer because dogs (and their owners) know she means business when she barks commands. Then Libby was to be lifted off the floor with one hand under her carrying her weight and the other on her scruff giving a motherlike pull. And finally she was to be isolated in a room by herself for about a minute.

The object of any punishment should be power not pain, and the pup's reaction to an angry leader should be submissive. Physical discipline however should be reserved for heinous crimes.

The children were told to make sure that she wasn't released from isolation when she was whining. We didn't want to teach her that whining could bring a reward! This routine is the simplest and most logical method of housetraining. Dogs are intensely social and one of the most effective psychological disciplines is temporary social isolation. Within a few days she had her favourite spots and we were able to move most of the paper. In part because she is a Golden Retriever, a 'houseproud' breed that dislikes soiling its own den, and in part because of the training routine, Libby was housetrained within days.

'That's how the 'I hate newspapers' game could have been avoided, but once an 'I hate . . .' game develops, there are ways of changing that too. The first rule is the most important. If a dog develops an 'I hate . . .' game do not think that it will just disappear on its own. It will not and it will need your help if it is to be corrected.

Knowing the original cause of an 'I hate . . .' game isn't really that necessary either, but you have to know what *stimulates* your pet's aggression. A game plan to change an 'I hate . . .' game goes like this.

1. Identify what it is that your pet hates (newspapers, umbrellas, visitors, etc.) and the environment where he usually plays the game. Some dogs will only play 'I hate . . .' in certain places. In Scruffy's case, we discovered that she hated newspapers more in the house than outside, which is frequently the case with the dog that hates visitors although not with dogs that hate other dogs.
2. Find out if there are similar objects that don't provoke your dog into playing 'I hate . . .' (Scruffy, for instance, hated newspapers but didn't mind magazines as much) or if there is a certain distance beyond which your dog is not induced to behave antisocially.

What do you mean, any closer and you won't be responsible for the saucepan?

3. Teach your dog to sit and stay on command. Even if you have done this before, go back to basics and practise the sit-stays, giving food rewards for at least a week. *This is most important.* You must exert leadership and authority and the dog must obey fully. If you do not spend enough time reinforcing the sit–stays, it is pointless to go on and you can forget about trying to change your pet's game. When your dog is 'guaranteed' trained, when it has learned to sit–stay for at least a minute, in return for praise and intermittent food rewards, he is ready to go on to the next stage, and so are you.

4. That next stage is for the hate object to be introduced to

the proceedings. Find the minimum distance that the dog
will respond to sit–stay commands when confronted with
the thing it hates before it shows signs of aggression. With
Scruffy, for example, if Mr Wallace sits down outside with
a newspaper and Mrs Wallace approaches to within five
metres with Scruffy on her lead and Scruffy willingly sits
and shows no signs of aggression, then she should be
rewarded with affection and a titbit. In Scruffy's case, to
begin with, a magazine was substituted for the newspaper.
(If you have a male dog and he hates other dogs, find a
friend who will let you use his female dog as the stooge
when you start your remedial training for this problem.)

5. Continue rewarding your dog for not playing 'I hate . . .'
   by rewarding his obedience and gradually, day by day,
   diminish the distance between the dog and the hated
   object.

6. At a certain point your dog will not respond passively to
   the presence of what it hates. *Do not use physical or verbal
   punishment*. This retraining should be pleasant for your dog,
   so when he reacts don't reward him with either food or
   affection but simply retreat to the previously successful
   distance and repeat the previous exercise over and over
   again – practise the sit–stays – until he is relaxed. Then
   give him his reward.

7. If your dog remains apprehensive even at the previous
   distance, keep retracing your steps until he no longer shows
   his 'I hate . . .' response. This means that on occasion you
   might have to take one step forward and two back. It's
   important, however, that each training session ends on a
   positive note, in a situation where the dog is performing
   passive sit–stays in return for a reward. This may mean
   that you will reach a critical point where progress can be
   measured in inches. *Do not despair*.

8. Training should be enjoyable for your dog. Don't tire him
   out or let him get bored with the training. Only train for the
   length of time that you know your dog will pay attention.

9. Training takes weeks and weeks but is successful if the owner is genuinely willing to devote the time that is necessary to alter an 'I hate . . .' game. 'Safe' responses have to be provoked literally hundreds of times before the pet's behaviour can be said to have changed for good.

'I hate . . .' games are among the most common aggression games that dogs play and with perseverance they can be altered using the method I have just described. But 'I hate . . .' games often aren't quite that simple. Many owners are content, even pleased, if their pets play 'I hate . . .' games.

OWNER: 'LOOK. I'M A LION TAMER'

'I'll pay you extra. Two hundred quid a dog if you do it. No one has to know. I'll help you with it after your nurses leave.' The owner was a heavy leather man, all tattooed arms and bulging muscles. His hair was cropped short at the back and at the sides. He had three Dobermanns; however he didn't look upon them as dogs but as weapons and he wanted me to be their technician, to crop their ears to make them look fiercer.

Ear cropping, cutting the ear to make it short and spiky, is an acceptable operation in North America and Germany but has been ethically unacceptable in Britain for years. It's of no value to the modern dog and is a senseless and unpleasant mutilation. Veterinary surgeons stopped doing it decades ago in the UK and this man knew it, but he was desperate to have his dogs' ears cropped so that they would look more aggressive. He was playing 'Look. I'm a lion tamer'.

The dogs were already pretty mean looking. All of them were scarred from fighting with each other and because of their short coats the permanent damage to the ears and necks was obvious. One of the dogs was too unreliable for me to examine it easily. If I just glanced at it, it stared back menacingly, then growled and snarled.

The owner had had those dogs since they were pups and played rough games with all of them to 'toughen them up'. The problem with his approach was that male Dobermanns toughen up on their own and need little help from us in that area. He fed them skinned sheeps' heads and let them fight over their food 'because it's natural for them' to do so.

This man's game was really a form of exhibitionism. 'Look. I'm a lion tamer' is supposed, in the mind of the player, to evoke a 'My goodness, how fierce and strong and manly you are' response from the game's observers.

There is an aspect of narcissism in most pet keeping, which is why the old adage that pets look like their owners is partly true. Most of the time we choose pets that compliment our personalities or at least the image that we have of ourselves. In that sense, a pet is really an extension of its owner. We can project our attitudes and feelings through the type of pet we have and what we will allow in the pet's behaviour.

Pets also represent what we would like to be, so that one person's fancy can be another person's anathema. Having a poodle that is kept immaculately cut will appeal to one person's pride and self-esteem. Having a careless-looking English Setter or Golden Retriever will appeal to another. This man's tough Dobermanns represented what he wanted to be like as much as his tatoos did.

Not all 'Look. I'm a lion tamer' games are bad games. Some people look upon the difficulties of training and managing a potentially lethal weapon as a challenge: the more others have given up, the greater the challenge to train the dog to be reliable and obedient. An older colleague of mine once said, 'Alsatians are like the Germans. They're either at your throat or at your feet.' The challenge of taking on one of these loaded guns with a cocked trigger and making it safe is one of the positive ways of playing 'Look. I'm a lion tamer'.

Some people feel a need to play castration games when they play 'Look. I'm a lion tamer'. Castration games between people are symbolic. With dogs they are for real!

Fritz bit Roger Dodds's ankles as he left the breakfast table once too often and now both Fritz and his owner were in my office and I was being given an ultimatum: either kill the Dachshund or castrate it. Fritz was a classic ankle-biter – a typical occupation of many of his compatriots. Dachshunds don't chase their quarry like other dogs, they ambush it, and although the genesis of Fritz's 'I hate ankles at the breakfast table' game was lost in the past, he would be instantly provoked into playing the game as soon as his victim put his morning paper down and uncrossed his legs. Fritz's eyes filled with rage, he muttered something to himself and then he attacked. Fritz was a small dog but as far as Roger Dodds was concerned, poison comes in small bottles.

Requests to castrate aggressive dogs can be based on a genuine misunderstanding of the effects of castration – of reducing the dog's level of male hormone. Castrating a dog will reduce urine marking activity, mating, roaming, mounting and aggression with other male dogs. Castrating a tomcat will diminish the likelihood that the cat will get into fights, mate, roam or spray. It will also ameliorate the unpleasant odour of tomcat's urine. But pet owners frequently harbour a fantasy that castration will make a dog less destructive, calmer, better with children and less aggressive to its owner.

It will not. If their canine's problem is that he has a predilection for humping green plastic frogs, then castration might be valuable. If they had wanted a dog that was less destructive, better with children, calmer and less aggressive with people, they should have got a bitch in the first place.

I explained these facts to Roger Dodds but he paid no notice. Though he might not have consciously realised it, he really wanted revenge and he was finally taking a stand, taking back the leadership he had relinquished to the dog. In a clumsy blunderbuss kind of way he was telling the dog that the breakfast table was now going to be his territory again. Unfortunately, his way of doing it would be ultimately unsuccessful.

If we had been in Sweden I could have invoked the law. There it is illegal to castrate dogs except under certain circumstances. But we weren't and I knew that Fritz's owner meant business. I suggested to Roger Dodds that he get another opinion and have not heard from him since.

3. TERRITORY GAMES

PET: 'GET LOST, BUSTER. I'M IN CHARGE HERE'

Once upon a time there was a Yorkshire Terrier named Fred. Fred was a tough nut. Like many of his breed he had, in spite of decades of inbreeding, maintained the Yorkie's basic terrier instincts to rape and pillage. He anointed every lampost, every hedge, every leaf, every blade of grass, every ant, proclaiming to all that cared to take a sniff, that this was Fred's territory. 'Prepare to meet your doom all ye who enter here,' he said with his urine.

Fred's territory marking was obsessive and he marked everywhere. It would have been more economical if he had been born with three legs, he kept one up in the air so long. Fred's ritual was to sniff, raise his left hind leg and deposit a drop of urine, thereby proclaiming the territory to be his, then

turn from north to south or east to west, but in all cases a full
180 degrees, lift his right hind leg and mark again. Then, as
my wife says, he 'bopped'; he kicked up some earth with his
hind legs (or regrettably some carpet or linoleum) leaving a
physical mark to his terrain. Fred suffered from territory
marking gone rampant and he was a nuisance whenever he
was brought in for me to examine him, for aside from his urine
marking proclivities he also protected his territory by barking
– and any territory he was standing on, as far as Fred was
concerned, was his.

I have a doorbell that clients have to ring and Fred's
territorial imperative would begin there. As deft as a cat
burglar and in full trot, he would leave his mark on the front
door, the hall wall and the door to reception. He was so quick,
even he probably didn't know how successful he was, and
without breaking stride he would anoint the leg of a chair and
the reception desk. Each time the doorbell rang he barked; he
barked to protect his territory. Some dogs sing, others yodel,
but barking is the commonest way a dog signals, 'This is my
place – get lost, buster.'

Fred barked when the doorbell rang and he barked when he
saw other visitors come into reception. I'm quite sure that
dogs have no idea of their size, and little dogs certainly don't.
Fred would challenge anything. All in all, between his barking
and urine marking he had earned a distinct mark on his
medical record card, a 'P'. Fred was a pest.

One day Fred was in reception while his owner waited for
me to see him and a Pyrenean Mountain Dog came in. Fred
danced at the end of his lead, barking, showing his teeth –
smiling, as Yorkie owners describe it – and creating his usual
obnoxious song and dance. His owner as always did nothing.
The Pyrenean looked perplexed. He was probably familiar
with fleas but this pipsqueak of an irritation looked, smelled
and sounded like a dog, a male dog. And what was the midget
trying to tell him? Was the little yapper actually saying, 'Get
lost, buster. This is *my* territory'? Did it really think that it

could defend the reception room as *his* territory? The Pyrenean stiffened and looked straight at Fred, but Fred's display remained ferocious and he yapped and lunged at the bigger dog. So the Pyrenean walked over to Fred and drowned him. He peed all over him. Not just a symbolic drop but a torrent, enough for Fred to still look like a soaked rat five minutes later when I got around to seeing him and he had already been dried off. Fred shut up like a clam because he inherently understood territory games and he knew he was up against a real winner. The Pyrenean might have been pretty nonchalant about his business but he was a master at playing 'Get lost, buster. I'm in charge here'.

Want a fight?

Territory games are among the most common that pets play. Ben, the Cocker Spaniel that forced his owners to retreat from their own bed and take up residence in the spare room, was playing a ritualised territory game. Territory games are played, very often in a ritualised fashion, to reassert a dog's position in the social order of its pack, or in other words, to gain recognition – to get 'stroked'.

A dog will defend its own territory, not only on behalf of itself but also on behalf of its other pack members: its family.

This is why a dog is so much more dangerous in its own home than it is off of its territory, at a veterinary clinic for example.

I make lots of house visits and I do so for a number of reasons. Sometimes they are unavoidable obligations, but they also get me out of the clinic, are a break from normal routine, and can be fun. Albert Finney became concerned about the well-being of a chicken he was playing opposite and asked me to visit the chicken on the roof of the West End theatre in which they were appearing. On the roof I found two chickens, the star and his understudy. The star, a cock, was emaciated and haggard but his understudy, who lived in the same coop with the star, was plump and well feathered . . . and a hen. It was spring and this feathered fiend was wasting away, using up all his energy on amorous pursuits.

Regardless of the reason for house visits, they almost invariably present greater problems when it comes to giving a good clinical examination. The dog or cat is on its own territory and knows how to hide successfully from the stranger as it defends itself and its territory. I don't know how many bedrooms I have been in where I have had to rearrange the furniture in order to examine the cat.

Dogs play 'Get lost, buster' by pursing their lips, raising their hackles, lowering their heads and threatening. Dobermanns are really good at this. I like Dobermanns because as a rule they are easy to read. Although I think there is probably no better dog than a superb German Shepherd, as a breed Shepherds are untrustworthy because so many of them are *angstbeisers*. There are too many quirky and unreliable ones for me to have faith in the breed. Dobermanns, on the other hand, are transparently what they are and their defence of territory, a natural canine trait, has been exaggerated in them through selective breeding. My only slightly serious physical injury occurred when I let my guard lapse once while I was on a house visit to attend to a Dobermann. I examined and inoculated the dog, then turned my back on him to write up his medical record. As I did he lunged for me and sank his teeth into my arm. It was winter when this happened and I was wearing a heavy padded overcoat, a jacket, a longsleeved sweater and a longsleeved flannel shirt, yet he still caused puncture wounds and bruising that was visible for several weeks. One of my nurses received far more serious injuries to both of her arms when she was attacked while holding a German Shepherd for me, an attack that could not be anticipated easily because the dog was a difficult one to 'read'.

Cats can play exquisite territory games too. The sense of grace of a cat, its sensuous beauty, its primitive unaltered wildness, is enough to put some cat owners into a poetic reverie and when these sensuous packages of power pee on their beds, owners find it pretty hard to handle. I'll be told by the owner of a cat that urinates in strange places that it does it out of 'spite', but the cat is really just playing a territory game, anxious that its territory is being threatened. Mr Moggs, a neutered tom, began spraying in his house, but through a careful history taking it transpired that another cat had recently appeared in Mr Moggs's back garden. Through devious means, the owners were able to scare the interloper away and, like Hamlet's father's ghost, Mr Moggs's peeing problem instantly vanished into the woodwork.

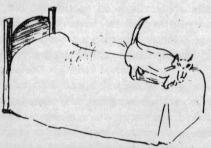

A whole week to establish territory, then wham — washday again

In a city like London dogs have to get used to car journeys and, aside from the stress games that they learn, this results in two common forms of 'Get lost, buster' territory games, barking and head bashing. (Car or bicycle chasing games, another variation of 'Get lost, buster', aren't frequently seen in London because so many dogs are kept on leads. In these games, dogs perceive moving objects as threatening and chase them. The fact that the car or bicycle actually 'runs away' reinforces the game and eventually ritualises it.)

The inside of a car is a nice neat territory for a dog to defend – enclosed, protected, den-like and almost always occupied by other members of his pack. It's a natural place to defend and even the gentlest, most reliable pet can unexpectedly become a glazed salivating monstrosity when a stranger approaches 'his' car and he's inside. John Steinbeck didn't know it when he wrote *Travels with Charley*, but he eloquently and humorously described a classic territory game. Steinbeck recounted driving with Charley into Yellowstone National Park in this way:

> Less than a mile from the entrance I saw a bear beside the road and it ambled out as though to flag me down. Instantly, a change came over Charley. He shrieked with rage. His lips flared, showing wicked teeth that had some trouble with a dog biscuit. He screeched insults at the bear . . . I have never been so astonished in my life. To the best of my knowledge, Charley had never seen a bear, and in his whole history had shown great tolerance for every living thing. Besides all this, Charley is a coward, so deep seated a coward that he has developed a technique for concealing it. And yet he showed every evidence of wanting to get out and murder a bear that outweighed him a thousand to one.

Even a dog as civilised as Charley can't help but play 'Get lost, buster' when the circumstances direct him to do so.

Owner: 'He'll Protect Me'

Cindy lived above a tailor's shop in Soho and it wasn't the first time I had visited her. Her place was easy to find and when a quick visit was necessary I would either walk over or take a bus along Oxford Street, get off and walk down the side street until I came to her name and doorbell. She had a long name for such a petite girl, 'Cindy Large Chest For Sale', and her front door was always open. She also had two young Dobermanns, in case she had any unfriendly visitors.

I knocked on her door and was admitted by an elderly Italian woman. I saw at once that the problem was the same as it always was, the dogs had attacked each other; they had had a territorial dispute and once more neither had won. Cindy came out of the other room and I saw that her arms were bruised and she had crêpe bandages on both wrists. 'I got those dogs to protect me but I think I need another to protect me from them,' she explained.

Cindy's profession exposes her (with apologies once more for an unavoidable pun) to danger and, like most of the other prostitutes I meet in London, she keeps a large dog for protection (although many of her co-workers have little dogs and cats as companions too). It's a wise move. A well-trained German Shepherd or Dobermann will deter many people if they think the dog will defend its master or protect its territory. Cindy's problem was twofold. The first was that the dogs were young and were spending all their time defending their territory against each other, and the second was that Cindy didn't look or sound like she had the mental ability to train herself, let alone the dogs. The dogs were out of control, and if one of them attacked a stranger it would probably do so on its own terms ('I don't like the smell of your aftershave') rather than on its owner's terms ('Help! Protect me'). (The episode created a territory game for me too. As I sat on Cindy's sofa seriously talking to her, her doorbell rang and in came another man. 'Dr Fogle!' he said. 'Fancy meeting *you* here!')

The image of the dog is loyalty to death but, as I explained in Chapter One, this is an image and not a fact. The image, however, leads to owners playing 'He'll protect me' games and raises an important question. Should a person feel responsible *for* a dog or *to* a dog? Many pet owners feel the latter, leading to so many of the problem games that people play with their pets.

Pets play games to win. They want to receive rewards and control situations. They want recognition. They want to be 'stroked'. Pet owners interpret their pets games in their own fashions to fulfil their own needs and fantasies. A pet owner might allow his pet to liberally roam the streets, 'to be free', because that's the way he would like to be. What he forgets is that rather than roaming idyllically like Huck Finn, his dream is misplaced and the dog will just act like a dog, mark out his territory with the pheromones in his urine and his anal sacs and then, depending on his dominance rating, either be recruited into a street gang or set one up himself.

Because 'He'll protect me' is such a common game, we often reinforce it without knowing it. Owners of the Freds and other little yappers of this world – the territorial dogs – often have a similar way of coping with their dog's territorial instincts. The doorbell rings and the dog barks and the owner's response to the bark, like a well-trained Pavlovian dog himself, is to pick up the dog. If the dog is a big one it is held by its collar, but invariably the dog is given contact comfort; it gets 'stroked'; its place in the order of things is reinforced. 'Don't be such a pain in the neck with your barking,' the owner might be verbally admonishing the pet, but his body language and his behaviour is saying, 'Good dog. Thank you for protecting me.' He is actually reinforcing the pet's undesirable territory game.

Dogs that play these territory games should be treated coldly and with aloofness. They need remedial education but it's just too much trouble for most pet owners to retrain their territory protectors. Owners of little dogs frequently find it easiest to just isolate the beasts in a locked room until their pet's blood stops boiling. Dogs might continue to mutter expletives under their breath for a while but then they calm down and, when released, come out and investigate the visitors. Don't forget, dogs are intensely social and even a stranger can be a social reward. When the dog is allowed out it should be disregarded by the owner. That directs the dog's needs for social activity to the visitor.

If you genuinely want to alter your dog's territorial protectiveness, use the game plan I outlined to alter a dog's aggressive 'I hate . . .' game (p. 96) but employ a few alterations. Once the dog is trained to sit–stay by your front door, arm a visitor with a food reward for your dog and get your visitor–stooge to ring the doorbell. As soon as the dog barks, force it to sit–stay, and when the visitor comes in, make sure that he doesn't look at the dog, speak to him or move abruptly but get him to toss the food reward to your dog, as long as the dog is being obedient.

Using the lead, allow your dog to investigate the visitor, preferably either outside the door or inside in another room but not actually at the front door, the place where his territorial protectiveness is at its maximum. While this investigation is going on the visitor should offer another food reward and act friendly – talking to you – and you should remain cold and aloof from your dog. If you persevere, it works.

Pet owners play a secret fantasy game with their pets – the homing game. It is a common fantasy that, regardless of the circumstances, a dog knows where his home is and come hell or Spaghetti Junction he will return to his own territory. Some of these stories seem to have a provenance which is difficult to dispute.

R. H. Smythe, a veterinary surgeon, recounted one of these stories half a century ago in his book *The Mind of a Dog*. He described how a Red Setter bitch named Dinah was sent from Cookstown to Lurgan in Ireland, a distance of about twenty-five miles by train. Shortly after her arrival Dinah produced a litter of five pups, but then disappeared. Ten days later she was found asleep in the old nest she had built in Cookstown, with all of her five pups alive and well, healthy and tucked in. Dinah's feet were raw and bleeding and she was dreadfully emaciated. To do what she had done, Dinah would have to have carried the pups in relays and have swum the river Blackwater, over seventy-five metres wide. Dinah recovered from the ordeal, reared her pups and remained at Cookstown. The story was told to Mr Smythe by a Professor Lamont of Belfast University. Dinah was his mother's dog.

There is something deep within us that makes us *want* to believe the story. We *want* to feel that our pets are immutably attached to their young, to us and to our homes. For years I believed that the story 'The Incredible Journey' was true, that a young Labrador, an old Bull Terrier and a Siamese cat overcame all adversities and, helping each other, journeyed hundreds of miles to finally return home. And I felt a loss when I learned it was not true. It was too good not to be true. I *wanted* to believe it just as so many movie-goers wanted to believe that Lassie would overcome all odds to return to her young master. We want to believe because that image of the dog, of faithfulness against all odds, is so profound in so many. It is, however, based on our symbolically seeing our pets as parents – caring, comforting and willing to die for us.

In practice I see dogs that have a homing influence more

closely related to the magnetic north pole or the scent of a
good meal than to inherent natural territorial ability. When a
client of mine once lost her Old English Sheepdog outside my
front door the day after I had spayed the dog she assumed that
the dog would return to her home, ten minutes south of my
practice, because the dog knew the territory. Maybe it was
because it was an Old English, a breed that never really does
learn to tie its own shoelaces, but this dog turned up two days
later, over fifteen miles away, in north-east London.

Cat owners respect, even revel in the independence of their
cats, which means that their homing instinct games are
inversions of dog owners' territory games although they serve
the same purpose. The games reinforce respect and admiration and love of the creature. A journalist client of mine, a
sensible, no-nonsense man who has a house full of cats
himself, recently told me a story about a fellow journalist's
cat, and once again the story takes place in Ireland.

The cat lived in a semi-isolated farmhouse with this man's
mother. (There may be significance in the fact that these
stories so often concern animals owned by the storyteller's
mother.) After a period of time, it took to making visits to a
neighbouring farm several fields away. The fields were
separated by stone walls typical of the area and the cat would
easily overcome these obtacles when it made its visits.

Although the visits were short to begin with, they became

longer and longer until a point was reached where the cat was spending more time away from home than at it. The owners, however, didn't interfere with the animal's activities and respected their cat's independence, although they regretted the loss of companionship. One day, the cat returned home and went directly to where it slept, picked up its blanket in its teeth and as the man's mother watched, dragged the blanket out of the house. She watched as it crossed the first field and the first stone wall, and then the next field and the next wall and finally, the last one. The cat and the blanket never returned.

Stories like these reinforce in owners' minds the roles that they want their pets to play. The territory game that dog owners want their dogs to play is diametrically opposite to the game that cat owners want their cats to play. If you want to find out whether you are a dog person or a cat person, think about which game appeals to you most. If you like them equally you will make a marvellous client for any veterinary surgeon!

CHAPTER FIVE

Living with People Games

1. DOMINANCE GAMES

PET: 'SIMON SAYS . . .'

Bomber was five years old when he saved his family from certain death. I had always known that he was a sensible dog but now he was a hero. After all, it said so in the papers. A loyal Labrador had smelled smoke and had gone into each of the three bedrooms of its house, awakening the occupants to the danger and enabling them to escape in their nightclothes. Bomber had acted the way all pet owners, in their fantasies, expect their pets to behave, but within a year Bomber had to be given away because he had learned to play a dangerous version of the children's game 'Simon says . . .'

Bomber was just right for learning this game – for learning how to take control of his owners and dictate terms. He knew better than his owners that dominance is one of the most important facets of the social life of dogs. He was big and strong and male, and although canine leaders are not always the biggest or toughest, it sure helps if you've got the muscles to psyche out the other members of your pack. All his life, Bomber had accepted his place in his pack's social structure. His owners and their two teenage sons were all of a higher social rank. They made the decisions and were his leaders. They decided when he should eat, what he should eat, where he should sleep, when he should be allowed freedom outdoors, and when he should 'speak'. But after the fire everything changed.

Bomber had raised the fire alarm by barking and in the following weeks, each time he barked he was praised. He was showered with gifts. Beef for breakfast. Lamb for lunch. Bomber was the centre of attention.

That was, in fact, the problem in a nutshell. Bomber got too much attention, he saw his opening and started moving up the totem pole. The way he did it was to demand attention and if he didn't get it, he bit. Bomber says, 'Feed me!' Bomber says, 'Let me out!' Bomber says, 'This is my bed now!' Bomber says, 'Don't touch that. It's mine!' Bomber says, 'Don't touch *me*!!'

Within weeks, this once amenable family Labrador had worked his way up the social order until he was above the teenage sons but below their parents. The sons were easy to dominate because they were the ones who were the most permissive and indulgent with Bomber after he had saved them. He was a fantasy hero who had become a real hero. And this was when Bomber was brought in for me to see. His owners wanted to know whether castration would make the dog easier to manage but I told them that it would be practically useless. Bomber didn't play dominance games with other dogs. He only played them with his human pack, the teenage sons and their parents.

I explained to his owners what the family would have to do in order to regain their dominance over the dog – how to be a tough drill sergeant – but they just couldn't bear to treat their hero that way, and eventually they were compelled to give him away.

Bomber was unusual in that he learned to play 'Simon says . . .' when he was already five years old. Most dogs learn how to play the game before they are eighteen months of age and, although the larger breeds like German Shepherds, Rottweilers and Labradors are the obvious candidates, any breed and all three sexes (male, female and neuter) can play it.

The American writer E. B. White once had a little dog that was a wizard at dominance games. White knew exactly what was going on and described his situation this way. 'For a number of years past,' he wrote, 'I have been agreeably encumbered by a very large and dissolute Dachshund named Fred. Of all the dogs whom I have served I've never known one who understood so much of what I say or held it in such deep contempt. When I address Fred I never have to raise either my voice or my hopes. He even disobeys me when I instruct him in something that he wants to do. And when I answer his peremptory scratch at the door and hold the door open for him to walk through, he stops in the middle and lights a cigarette, just to hold me up.'

'My dog cheats and steals,' she said, paraphrasing Mr White but showing exasperation with her pet rather than resignation. And she was right. Her miniature poodle Cindy was staring straight at me: eyeball-to-eyeball contact. A little black ball of fluff with a pink ribbon in its hair was trying to shake me up.

Cindy's instinct to dominate was there from birth; she was a highly independent dog but those instincts hadn't been inhibited when she was young because her owner was a very nurturing person; an emotional pushover for 'Simon says . . .' games. It was a miserable relationship. The owner had become a doormat for her dog. It had trained her, although that isn't always the case. One of the most intriguing aspects of 'Simon says . . .' is that the game may be played under one set of circumstances but not under another. A dog may wear a halo in its own home but develop horns and a spiked tail in a car. It may win the Nobel Peace Prize at dog training classes but be an urban terrorist on the streets. It may be a bowl of jelly with friends or strangers but turn into a werewolf to protect its food. 'Simon says . . .' is a game that is usually played in highly specific circumstances or situations.

pathetic – she can never
tell when I'm joking

Chasing cars is a classic 'Simon says . . .' game although it may not initially appear to be one. Look at it from the dog's point of view. A pup may be frightened by a big moving car, or a bicycle for that matter, so it barks at it. Simon says, 'Go away!' *and it does*! It doesn't take even the foggiest dog very long to realise that this is a very effective game. Show dominance, protect your territory, bark, chase. It works! And the behaviour is reinforced each time the game is played because each time the dog barks and chases a car, the car runs away.

One of the commonest 'Simon says . . .' games is Simon says, 'Don't brush me.' A dog might be a perfect angel most of the time but as soon as it sees a brush it becomes a demon. 'If you come one step closer with that brush,' it says with its eyes and lips and ears. 'If you move another inch, I'll tear you to pieces. I'll make mincemeat out of you. And I'll never be your friend again.' At least that's how most owners see it.

There are two ways to treat 'Simon says . . .' dominance games; prevention in the first instance, or cure if the game has developed.

It's not possible to overemphasise the importance of the early training of a pup, because if that training is carried out effectively you will be able to control most, if not all, 'Simon says . . .' games. Some owners feel that they should use a permissive approach in the rearing of their pups; that they avoided heavy discipline with their children and produced offspring they are proud of and want to do the same with their dog. Well, the first rule is that a Yorkshire Terrier isn't one of the kids. It has to be treated like a dog – in a way that a dog will understand. That means that *you* are the one who plays 'Simon says . . .'

When a pup is first taught its name, it should also be taught to sit. I did it with Liberty this way. During the first days that we had her, when she was eight weeks old, we discovered that like most pups she went mad over yeast-flavoured vitamin tablets, so I used these as rewards in her initial training. With one hand I would push down her rump into the sitting position while my other hand holding the treat was raised directly above her head in such a way that the most comfortable position for her to look at that hand was a sitting one. While doing this I said, 'Sit.' After a few tries, just moving my hand over her head and saying 'Sit' made her do so, and finally the word alone was sufficient.

This is just about the most important thing you can teach your dog because it sets the relationship between you and your pet for life. The social psychologist will call the dog's response 'compliance' and in compliance, power is the most important component; power to praise, to give love, to scream, to discipline, to withhold exercise, to open the car door or to play fetch. If you have that power then you can play other games with your pet with the foreknowledge that *you* hold the power to say, 'Enough!'

Cindy, the miniature poodle that cheats and steals, never learned to comply, never learned that her owner was her leader, because she wasn't. She wasn't because when the dog was young she didn't exert any authority over it. She allowed her dog to play 'Simon says . . .' I see lots of people who succumb to the game and I'll describe them in Submission Games (pp. 126–35). Dogs *need* discipline when they are young. They need to *know* they will be disciplined for playing 'Simon says . . .' Dogs will try to dominate by pulling on their leads, running away, barking, biting, growling, nipping, chasing and charging. The dominant dog that isn't taught obedience as a pup can end up doing all of these things and is then brought to me as if I, through some miracle cure, can do something about it. These are the pets that have turned their owners into the true housepets, but there is still hope as long as the owner is willing to reassume the dominant role in the pack.

Your game plan should follow these points. First of all prepare a list of when and where your pet plays 'Simon says . . .' Dominance games are very often specific to certain

locations or certain people. Folks are routinely amazed that I can clip Sparky's nails while he is on my examining table and tell me with incredulity in their voices that if they try at home Sparky becomes the Creature from the Black Lagoon. Pets usually have an order of environments in which they are most likely to play dominance games and it is important to work out where the dog is least amenable to brushing, clipping or whatever, and where he is most amenable to your dominance over him.

Now, let's say that through trial and error you discover that the dog most actively resents grooming in the living room and bedroom but is not as resentful in the back garden. This is what to do and it's all done to reinforce submissive behaviour in your dog.

1. Stop all petting of your dog except as a reward for correct behaviour. (That's pretty tough to do, and if you are playing an attachment game like 'He needs me' with your pet, it will probably be impossible to do.) From now on petting should only be used to reinforce submissive behaviour.

2. Retrain your dog to sit and lie down as I have just described in my training of Liberty (p. 119).

3. Isolate your dog from human company whenever he shows any sign of aggression. This means putting him in an empty room (empty of people, that is) for one or two minutes whenever he challenges your authority.

4. To impose social isolation safely, leave your dog's collar and lead on at all times, indoors and out. Trailing the lead all the time will in its own way subdue your dog, at least for the first few days, but it will also give you a safe way of implementing 'quiet time'.

5. In the garden, where your dog has been least resentful of brushing, command him to sit and lie down, then gently brush him for a few seconds. If he submits to the grooming, reward him with petting. *If* he rebels, isolate him for a few minutes.

6. Repeat this exercise daily until you can safely brush him in the easiest environment (the garden) finally working your way to the most difficult environment (for example, the bedroom).

During all of this retraining you have to keep a sharp lookout for any fifth column activity – a husband or wife or child who is surreptitiously tickling or feeding the monster. To reassert dominance you've got to be ruthless and tough.

Some pet owners can unfortunately be ruthless and tough on their pets not because it is a necessity but because they have their own personal reasons for wanting to dominate something. A pet can be an easy answer.

Owner: 'Just Remember, Rex, I'm the Boss'

Pet owners will play dominance games with their pets for five reasons. Some owners dominate animals as a way of getting attention. The tattooed man with the Dobermanns who played 'Look. I'm a lion tamer' is, through his supremacy over his two fierce-looking dogs, fulfilling his need for attention. This might be a harmless outlet for his own personal needs – a vent for his personal type of exhibitionism – but it is not always healthy for the animals.

Other pet owners will dominate their pets for revenge. Direct revenge occurs when owners of dogs like Fritz, the

Dachshund that plays 'I hate ankles at the breakfast table', overreact to their dog's odious habits, as Fritz's owner did, and bring their pets to me demanding castration or summary execution. People can also play their revenge games through their pets. They use their dogs and cats, their control of the animals, as a way of getting at the person they really want to dominate. These are usually husband and wife games in which the pet is the innocent caught in the middle and which I will describe in the next chapter under the subject of Scapegoat Games (p. 175).

A third reason that some people will exhibit dominance over an animal is to compensate for a genuine fear of the beast. Their problem is that they are really frightened of the animal and overcompensate by trying to become bullies. I'll discuss this next, in this chapter, under Submission Games (p. 126).

The fourth reason for dominance games is divine right. The Bible gives man 'dominion over fish, fowl, cattle and every living thing'. The philosopher René Descartes took this notion to its logical extreme and taught that animals are simply machines over which we have complete control. That idea conveniently overlooks the fact that the higher animals, and this certainly includes dogs, have intelligence, self-awareness, lateral thought and, who knows, maybe even a conscience too. We might be the dominant intelligence on this planet but our conceit in that knowledge would be laughable to any other species clever enough to appreciate it.

That leaves the final reason for playing 'I'm the boss' – power! Dominating your pet out of fear, or to get revenge, or because it is man's right, or to get attention, is unhealthy. But dominating your pet for power is acceptable and correct as long as you do so for the right reasons. Power is the most important component in compliance; power to praise, to give love, to scream, to discipline. The basis for a healthy relationship between a person and a pet is that the human is the animal who holds the power. Ask any veterinary surgeon,

ROVER!

His master's Bank

however, and he or she will tell you that, in many instances, this is but a wishful fantasy.

Liberty, my Golden Retriever, is, I'm afraid, a bit of a renegade. She listens to commands, processes them through her defective computer and goes for a swim anyway. Then she comes back and apologises. She's a classic give-her-an-inch-and-she'll-take-a-mile type of dog. (One of my kids is just like her.)

When we named her we immediately found ourselves shortening Liberty to Libby. After all, she was at that time a soft, cuddly, affectionate pup. But as she grew and as her true personality developed, I noticed that my wife insidiously, and certainly without realising it, changed the dog's name. First she stopped calling her Libby and reverted to Liberty; by the time the dog was ten months old and her wayward personality had become apparent her name had changed to Bert. It had done so because, sloppy and soft as the dog might look, she needed firm handling: she was an innate housedog and power was necessary to dominate her. Her territorial protectiveness was masculine. She was a Bert, not a Libby, and to Julia it simply instinctively sounded better to exert discipline – to show power – to exhibit dominance to the degree it was needed – over something that was masculine rather than feminine.

All pet owners must play power games to control their pets. The owner takes on the position of leader of the pack, the most powerful position, and through the judicial use of power dominates the dog and lets it know that its social position within the family is at the bottom of the pile. People who play 'I'm the boss' correctly do so with firmness but with compassion. Power can corrupt, however, even in the hands of pet owners, and this is when dominance games get out of control.

In all animals dominance is established and maintained by some form of aggression or coercion, and although this is necessary if a pet owner is to successfully exert power over his dog, it can get out of hand.

Mr Smith's Springer Spaniel had a dislocated hip and severe bruising over its hind quarters. The dog's groin was red and tender and tense to the touch and he found it painfully difficult to move. His injuries were recent, consistent with being hit by a car, but Mr Smith was candidly honest with me. 'He went for me and I kicked the shit out of him,' he explained.

In some people the need to dominate assumes greater importance in their personality make-up than the need for affection, and these are the pet owners who punish their pets mercilessly. But this wasn't the reason that Mr Smith had beaten his dog so. He was deeply upset at what he had done, which was why he brought Ferret in to me so quickly, and although he tried to appear rational and level-headed as he explained exactly what had happened, it was obvious that he felt like an incompetent second-rate fool.

Mr Smith is a financial consultant in the City and Ferret is his working gun dog. Mr Smith's job demands that he appears to be responsible and competent; that he has all the trappings of power. Which is in part why he beat his dog so. Think about the words that you associate with the competent, responsible and powerful person. Level-headed, rational, strong, mature, unemotional, tough. This is the image that this man had to maintain at all times. He had to project strength. It is, in fact, the stereotype 'male' image, and it's interesting that men can carry this image over into their relationships with animals. Men are more punitive and less affectionate with horses than women are, for example. In Mr Smith's business, a warm, expressive and affectionate personality would promote the wrong image. Those are not the facets of power. Those are 'female' stereotypes and are associated with impracticality, self-indulgence and emotion.

Mr Smith is in fact a powerful man within the London financial community, but in order to attain and retain that position he has had to not just play but live 'I'm the boss' twenty-four hours a day. And when his dog snarled at him, his reaction was power in excess. (Mr Smith's problem is not his alone. Veterinary surgeons play the same game for the same reasons, only in different ways. Many, perhaps most, vets dare not show their true feelings when they speak to clients because they want to maintain the trappings of authority and power; they want to appear completely competent. Women veterinary surgeons fall into the trap of mimicking their male colleagues by assuming the male stereotype to show their authority. Many women play 'I'm the boss' simply by acting like men and, male or female, this need to show power and authority is why so many professionals present such unfeeling exteriors.)

Mr Smith used power in excess because the image he had to convey for his business completely dominated his life, but his true personality showed through in the fact that he had instantly brought his dog in for me to attend to and, as frequently happens in the vet's consulting room, by his open and honest explanation of how he felt.

He asked to stay while I anaesthetised Ferret, repaired the dislocation and treated the wounds. 'I feel like a fool,' he told me. 'I've had dogs all my life and have never done such a thing.' And it was true that I never expected such an apparently intelligent man to abuse his dog so. He was big enough to be transparently honest to me, but he was also racked with guilt and rightly worried about how his abuse of power would affect the working relationship he had with his dog. A working dog needs to feel a certain amount of independence and he wondered whether Ferret would be fearful of him and become cowering and submissive, although as events transpired he did not. Dogs will play submission games out of fear or innate shyness. They will also play submission games that aren't submission games at all, which is what I will discuss next.

2. SUBMISSION GAMES

Pet: 'Hold Me – Protect Me – Care for Me'

Everyone always feels sorry for Jasper. He's a full-grown German Shepherd now but he's still car sick each time he's taken out for a journey. And he goes off the deep end if the reason for the journey is a visit to the dreaded vet. He arrives simply oozing saliva. A pool forms on the floor in front of him within minutes of his arrival. If he is delayed in reception too long a larger, more pungent pool appears on the floor between his legs. Jasper whimpers and constantly looks at his owner, trying to get on her lap. 'Hold me – Protect me,' he says with his eyes and with his actions. Sometimes he does manage to get on his owner's lap and I'm sure that other folks in reception no doubt go home and later over dinner regale their families with implausible stories about macho German Shepherds at the vet's sitting on ladies' laps: teddy bears in wolves' clothing.

Jasper cowers when I examine him. So do I a bit because Jasper is an *angstbeiser* – a nervous biter – and is apprehensive of any contact with strangers. In the summer I usually have to treat him for moist spots of skin infection that are secondary to self-inflicted skin damage, which he hates because each 'hot spot' has to be thoroughly scrubbed. Jasper is a classic submissive dog, a big dog that would prefer to be carried by his leader-owner, a dog that begs for protection. His carsickness, his salivating, his urinating on the floor, his fear, his shyness, his self-inflicted wounds, even his untalked-about masturbation in the privacy of his own kennel, are all signs of the submissive dog.

I've taught him to cringe on command

All dogs must be trained to be submissive to their human bosses if they are to be socially acceptable within the community, no dog should be the leader of the pack. But submission can be inflicted rather than instructed and the unpleasant, even heartrending results are the Jaspers of dogdom.

Years ago I did a routine ovariohysterectomy on an exceptionally frightened and nervous German Shepherd bitch. She was the most apprehensive animal I had ever treated and during the day she was with me my staff discovered that her owners kept her locked in their storeroom at their place of work, ostensibly to guard the liquor and cigarettes from staff pilferage. I could only guess at how she had become so nervous and agitated, and once I knew about the way she lived I refused to let the owners take her home. Her owners threatened to bring in the police to get their dog back and I told them gleefully to go ahead. There are good laws in England to enforce humane treatment of animals. I won. They backed down but I was now stuck with a shivering hulk of teeth and muscles that I couldn't get within six feet of without the dog telling me to vanish or risk permanent injury.

I spread newspaper on the floor of a then empty room and started feeding her. On the first day she wouldn't eat in my presence but by the third day I could crouch down in the same room with her and talk to her as she ate. On the fifth day I was sufficiently confident to try to stroke her as she ate – and immediately regretted my haste. As she ate her food I talked soothingly, all the time looking away from her, avoiding threatening eye contact, but the instant I touched her hair she wheeled around and sank her teeth into my thigh. Then she apologised.

She collapsed defenceless on the floor, raised one leg in the air and urinated. I spoke to her calmly and stroked her again, she got up and with her ears in the 'friendly' back position she drowned me with licks, leaning into my body. From that day on she greeted me like her best friend, her leader, her boss dog. I had to keep my greetings low-key because her submissive urination was a nuisance to clean up, but by crouching down when I saw her, by stroking her under her chin rather than a more dominant pat on the head, and by keeping my movements gentle, her puppy-like submissive wetting quickly stopped. Her confidence was building up.

This dog was submissive for several reasons. First of all she was a German Shepherd, a breed that is surprisingly extreme in its behaviour, the breed that my colleague Frank Manolson once described as being either 'at your throat or at your feet'. But there is, as I have mentioned earlier, more to instinct than just genes, as was discovered recently in Sweden. The National Dog Training Centre in Sweden is responsible for training dogs for all types of service work, sniffer dogs, attack

It's a love token, really

dogs, dogs for the blind, etc., and they were, naturally enough, interested in the genetics of certain behaviour characteristics. Their discovery was that for many behaviour patterns the effect of the mother was much greater than the effect of the father. In other words, it wasn't just the genes that determined behaviour.

It has been known for years that if a newborn baby is immediately placed on its mother's belly right after birth and allowed to lie there for fifteen minutes, that baby will probably sleep sounder, cry less and learn to stand earlier than other babies. This type of imprinting of behaviour occurs in dogs too, and behavioural characteristics such as the need for contact, whining, fetch activity, object investigation and crying are influenced by the mother more than by the father. This is an intriguing discovery because it means that once imprinting is better understood it should be possible to determine which bitches will be the most suitable mothers for service dogs. The Shepherd bitch I was landed with might have had a lousy mother!

Finally and regrettably, this poor dog found itself in the wrong home. In fact it didn't have a home at all, it had a dark jail. Dogs can't endure long periods of isolation. They need lots of social activity. They need play experience. They need a social life. The ones that don't get that grow up as rogue dogs and usually submissive ones at that.

Jasper, the peeing Shepherd with the hot spots, the dog that wanted to be carried, was left alone each day while his owners went to work. They shouldn't have had a dog in the first place (or if they must they should have had two) and they tried to compensate for their being away by giving the dog treats and organising the most expensive training classes for him. But the dog that lives in a luxury jail, allowed out for walkies a few times a day, is the dog that develops a deep dependent submissive attachment for its owner. These are the dogs that develop Oedipus complexes with their leader-owners; the ones that are fawning, pathetic, apologetic wimps.

Their owners often love it. They revel in their dog's subservience, their dog's need for affection, need for protection, need for praise. And in their own ways these dogs are dominating their owners through their subservience. They are parasitising on their owner's need to nurture. Jasper's owner couldn't have spelled it out more lucidly than when she last brought him in for a routine booster inoculation. As Jasper panicked on the floor, virtually fainting at the sight of the syringe and needle, his owner knelt down and gently scruffed him and with love in her eyes and undoubtedly in her heart, she looked into his eyes and said, 'You are the least courageous person I know but I love you.' And then, after I had finished and Jasper was dancing at the door to leave, she looked at him again and said, 'Come on, child. Let's go.'

I ended up keeping the Shepherd bitch for another two weeks, during which time my nurses found it a new home in one of the suburbs. She's still there, an elderly lady now, still apprehensive, still acting as a good housedog, but living with sensible people who have a common sense attitude towards her. Their business is also their home and the dog has given them security for over ten years. In return they have given the dog the security of authority figures – leaders. A happy ending.

OWNER: 'HOLD ME – PROTECT ME – STAY WITH ME'

By now you should be asking yourself, and with justification, why people let their pets play some of these games. Why did the owners of the Cocker Spaniel Ben allow him to sleep on their bed? For that matter, why do half of the pet owners in London allow their pets to sleep in their bedrooms? Why do owners put up with constant bites from their pets and still love the beasts? Why do so many owners put up with 'Simon says . . .' games from their pets? Why are so many owners so downright submissive with their animals?

The explanation, in part, lies far in the distant past. Almost all of our evolutionary development occurred in the jungle and on the savannah, not in urban conurbations, and this development occurred while we lived an interrelated existence with other animals. All the social species of mammals, of which we are only one, evolved this way, which can explain why some of our responses to our pets do not always appear to be rational.

Eliot Aronson, a social psychologist, has translated this idea into Aronson's First Law, which says, 'People who do crazy things are not necessarily crazy.' Ben's owners aren't crazy, nor are the other pet owners who let their pets sleep with them. One of the reasons they let Ben sleep in their bedroom in the first place is buried deep in the primitive past. Ben's sleeping in the bedroom gives a signal of safety, a primitive instinctive sign that all is well. Biologically built into all of us is the fact that undisturbed living things have a calming influence on us. It doesn't matter if it's a gently swaying wheatfield or slowly moving clouds or animals quietly grazing or sleeping, our primitive response to these sights and sounds is a feeling of security. After all, the sight of animals resting has been a useful signal of safety throughout all of human evolution. I've experienced the feeling myself with my dogs.

My Golden Retriever Honey slept in her basket in our room all her life. During her final year Honey was an old crock. She didn't lie down in her whicker basket, she collided with it like a dropped brick. And if the humidity in the room was anything above fifteen per cent she panted so loud our whole bed vibrated. Sometimes between one end and another she smelled like a fish-littered seashore at low tide. If she woke up suddenly you could see that for the first minute she was in Never-never Land, and when she was in the land of nod, the 1812 Overture couldn't awaken her. She was as deaf as a doorpost. It's irrational to say that this geriatric of a dog gave us a feeling of calm or well being but she did.

Honey's young successor Liberty, who now shares our bedroom and has her own basket, gives us a feeling of security for another reason. When Libby hears the slightest noise downstairs she wakes up. When she hears anything more she woofs. It gives us an enhanced feeling of being protected. It gives my teenage daughter trying to tiptoe in at two a.m. a headache!

There are other reasons why we play submissive games with our pets, but because these are symbolic reasons they can be more difficult to either appreciate or understand.

Earlier on I explained how pets play a symbolic role in their owners' lives and how symbolically, silly as it sounds, pets act as parents. They act as parents because they are the lineal descendants of the transitional objects, the satin-edged blanket, the favourite soft bed toy, the icons we have created, that serve to bridge the gap that develops as we grow and separate from our parents early in life. Pets give contact comfort. Your blood pressure actually drops when you stroke your pet. Pets make you feel less lonely and more secure. Your state of arousal is diminished when you are in the presence of your own pet. That is what transitional objects do too. The family pet is symbolically a transitional object and gives some of the same rewards as the satin-edged blanket and the stuffed toy did when we were infants.

Constance Perin, a cultural anthropologist, once wrote about the 'superabundant love' that some people feel for their pets, a love that is so great that there are no possible human recipients. I come across this superabundant love almost daily when seemingly sensible people make seemingly senseless statements like, 'I love my dog more than my kids.' Outwardly that seems to be an impossibility. Your kids are your genes. Your dog isn't even the same species, let alone a relative. Yet people melt into butter with their pets. I like the way one pet owner recently described her relationship with her pet: 'I'm putty in her paws,' she told me.

We already know that pets are attachment figures. John Bowlby, in his book *Attachment*, explained the 'terrible twos' in children this way. He said that, 'So long as a child is in the unchallenged presence of a principal attachment figure, or within easy reach, he feels secure. A threat of loss creates anxiety and actual loss sorrow; both moreover are likely to arouse anger.' Primary attachment with mother, or what the British psychologist D. W. Winnicott calls 'merger with mother', starts to end at about two when the infant begins to realise that he is a separate being, a distinct entity. But this separation is an aching loss. The most important early ballast in life must be left behind.

I see lots of grown-ups who suffer the 'terrible twos' when it comes to their relationships with their pets, leading to the serious separation games I see; owners unwilling to leave their pets with me even for life-saving surgery. It is also the root cause of 'Hold me – Protect me – Care for me' submission games. To these people the pet symbolically plays the role of the all-powerful and perfect parent, and separation from the parent results in a feeling of helplessness. Constance Perin says that deep in our subconscious we also carry the anger we felt when 'merger with mother' ended; the anger we felt

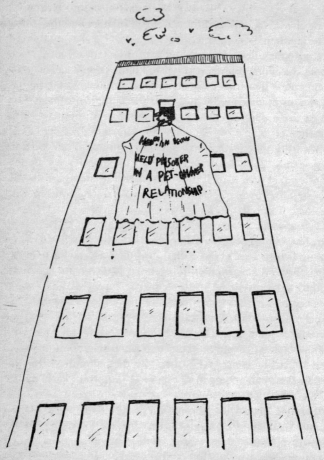

during the 'terrible twos'. And because dogs are symbolic parents, we also unconsciously show our anger in our relationship with them by exposing them to possible harm. It's a difficult concept to grasp, certainly for someone like myself who deals with the concrete and the absolute every day, but I acknowledge its validity.

Be that as it may, pet owners describe their pets in the terms of a love that is quite impossible to experience with fellow humans – complete – utter – total – immutable – lifelong – unending. 'He would die for me.' It is a love that is impossible in any human relationship and a love for which, in return, many owners are hopelessly and helplessly grateful. It is also a love that some pet owners become dependent upon. It is their drug. They need it because for them it is a purer love than they can find elsewhere. They become addicted to it and submit to their pet's demands for fear of losing it.

3. MANIPULATION GAMES

PET: 'TAKE NOTICE, I'M UPSET'

John knew from his wife's scream what had happened. She was in the kitchen about to fry an omelette for them both when he heard her blood-curdling cry. The phantom urinator had struck again!

This time it was in the frying pan but it wasn't the first time that the phantom had used that receptacle. The first time he had struck there John's wife hadn't exactly realised what the liquid was and the consequences were a bit more discomfiting. John himself had only recently endured the consequences of a visit by the phantom when a board meeting of his company's directors had had to be recessed for fifteen minutes after he had simply opened his briefcase. The phantom had secretly left his considerable mark on John's marketing report to his fellow directors.

The phantom had struck elsewhere too – in the bathtub and in the sink – and although he was called the phantom because the dirty deeds were never seen being perpetrated, John and his wife knew exactly who he was. And that's why Charlie was now on my examining table. Charlie, an affectionate, intelligent, neutered eighteen-month-old Siamese cat was the phantom and he was with me because his owners could cope no longer. Secretly I wondered how they had coped with his behaviour for so long!

The history that they gave me was quite specific for a manipulation type of problem, but there are many medical reasons why a cat will pee in the house and these had to be eliminated first. The most likely cause of behaviour like Charlie's is a bladder infection with a consequent burning sensation and need to urinate. For some reason, when cats suffer from cystitis they often empty their bladders in strange places like sinks and bathtubs.

A less likely but still common reason for the behaviour is anal gland discomfort. Blocked or infected anal glands, even though they are on either side of the anus, can predispose a tomcat to urinate in strange places.

Once these and other disease processes were eliminated, Charlie's owners had to face the fact that he was manipulating them in the best way he knew how.

Cats aren't the only pets that play the game. Dogs are equally adept at it. Hamish, a fifteen-month-old West Highland White Terrier, was brought in and positioned on my examining table with equal disgust. 'He's using us,' said Mrs Green. 'He doesn't like the sleeping arrangements we have made for him and he's getting back at us.' Hamish's problem was of more substance than Charlie's. He left neat piles of his droppings in the kitchen each night. He never did so if he was allowed to sleep in his owners' bedroom at night and he never did it when he and his owners went on holiday. Both Hamish and Charlie were in their own ways trying to let their owners know that they were upset with some aspect of their lives, trying to get their owners to take notice.

Cause and effect had already been determined in Hamish's case. He urinated only in the kitchen and only at night if he had to sleep there. He had said, 'Take notice, I'm upset,' and his owners had brought him to me for advice. Once I had eliminated the possible medical reasons for his behaviour I simply gave the owners retraining advice.

In Charlie's case the problem was more difficult to determine. If Charlie had had another cat living in his house and if that other cat had disappeared, then this would have been a sufficient cause for a personality change. But he hadn't. If Charlie's owners had recently redecorated or even moved the furniture around, that could be sufficient cause for him to pee in the briefcase on the marketing report. But they hadn't. If Charlie's owners didn't empty his litter tray often enough or if they had changed the position of his tray, or if it was too close to his feeding area, or if it was a new tray or if they were using a new litter, then he might show his distress by peeing in frying pans. But they didn't and hadn't. Charlie was saying, 'Take notice, I'm upset,' but on the surface it was impossible to understand why.

Charlie had been neutered when he was six months old (and before he had reached puberty) so he hadn't developed a tomcat spraying routine, but there were a few clues about his behaviour that were important. The previous spring, when he was a kitten, he had been allowed outdoors. Being agile and inquisitive, he had scaled the fence and disappeared. His owners found him the next day at their veterinary clinic. Charlie had probably been hit by a car and after that they didn't let him outside.

Spring came around once more and when asked, Charlie's owners told me that he spent a lot of time at the back window staring outside. In retrospect that was the most important information they gave me because, on my advice, they allowed Charlie to go out in their back garden again and as if by magic the phantom problem disappeared. His urinating in the house stopped.

There is a logic to Charlie's behaviour. Even though he was castrated the pituitary gland at the base of his brain was still producing stimulating hormones, and these hormones are most active in the spring. That's why even neutered cats will still spray. (Every veterinary surgeon will be approached by an irate client at least once each spring who says, 'You didn't do it properly. He's still behaving like an intact male.' That's because removing the testicles will eliminate undesirable sex behaviour and odour in most tomcats but deep down inside in the recesses of their pituitary glands they are still profoundly male.) Spring had arrived and so had Charlie's biological urge to create a territory, and inside the house was not where he wanted to be.

Once Charlie's elimination behaviour had reverted to an acceptable state his owners installed a sign over his litter tray. It was that old saw, eminently appropriate under the prevailing circumstances, 'We aim to please. You aim too, please.'

Pets will play manipulation games by leaving their calling cards in unwanted places, but it is questionable whether it is done through any abstract thought process. I am quite certain, however, that dogs and cats can form mental images. These may not be the same as yours and mine but it's pious to think that only humans can do so. Scientifically it can't be proven that pets can form mental images but why, for example, do dogs commonly have 'chasing dreams'? Why will a dog, as I described in Eating Games, show his desire for food by picking up his food bowl and dropping it at his owner's feet? I remember watching a sheepdog, blind in one eye, working some sheep on a televised sheepdog trial. The dog and sheep were in a gully, the sheep out of sight of the shepherd and the dog with his blind eye to him. The shepherd whistled his signal to the dog but because of the terrain he gave the wrong signal. The ever obedient dog disobeyed the signal, went around the appropriate way and brought the sheep in. On the same programme another dog was having difficulty getting a recalcitrant ewe to join a flock. After several tries the dog went back to the main flock, cut out three others and herded them to the recalcitrant ewe, then brought that group back to the main flock. It seemed to be a logical thought out process.

But how far do these images go? Consider this story, told to me by a respected London journalist. It concerns a seven-week-old female kitten that he found abandoned and that he took into his already cat-filled home. I'll quote from mid-letter.

We took her in, she domesticated very easily and she soon became very much my cat. We have five others already, however, and I eventually determined to find a good home for her and give her away.

[Now, this is the bit that's hard to believe.] From the day I determined to give her away, each morning she'd wake me up by jumping upon the bed and urinating on me. On my shins, to be precise. Each morning I'd come bang awake with my shins burning rather acidically. After about a week of this, it occurred to me that I couldn't give away such a 'dirty' cat and decided to keep her and somehow resolve the piss problem. Except there was no longer a piss problem! From the moment I decided to keep her, she stopped doing it. I'm not lightly given to ascribing intelligence to animals but it seems that the cat must have somehow picked up my change of attitude towards her – to give her away and then not to – and she responded accordingly.

Is it a manipulation game on the part of the cat or is it a guilt game on the part of the owner? Guilt games follow in the next chapter but before I discuss these I should mention the simplest, most common, but least recognised way in which pet owners play manipulation games: through the naming of their pets.

OWNER: 'I NAME THEE SIR O'GATE'

My Golden Retriever's full name is Liberty Olympia Sweetpea Chewing Fogle and I've already explained how her name gradually changed to Bert, but I haven't explained the full significance of all her names yet. The way we name our dogs and the way we breed them in the first place are our most subtle but also our most overt ways of manipulating our pets.

My family didn't name our dog Duchess, for example, because we weren't looking for a dignified or regal pet. We didn't name her Blitz or Panzer or Fang because we hadn't intended her personality to be aggressive or defensive. We didn't call her Scruffy or Grot because we didn't intend for her to be a vagabond. And we didn't call her Susie or Sally or Judy or Jane because we intentionally wanted to maintain some symbolic distance between her and the rest of the family. We wanted her to be the dog in the family, not another human.

In that last instance my family is in a minority. The most common type of name for a pet today is a human name. It's understandable because most pet owners ascribe human feelings and emotions to their pets and treat them as members of the family. People tell me that their dogs are poised, assured, stoic, reserved, phlegmatic, withdrawn, happy-go-lucky, outgoing and most important, a real baby. There is no denying that many pet owners treat their pets as children. That's why the Pekinese that had bad dreams was named Baby and why the raucous noisy poodles were named Candy and Sweetie.

It's really quite easy to see why. Most pets need grooming, and this reinforces parenthood. They need to be protected, and this reinforces parenthood. They are dependent on us for food, and this reinforces parenthood. We take this role one step further and physically manipulate our pets through selective breeding in order to perpetuate the childlike state of their behaviour. Many of the smaller breeds have been developed in such a way that the animals are perpetual emotional infants and these are often the dogs that are given human names – Jasper, Willy, Cindy, Tracy.

Yoo-hoo Cuthbert... Cuthbert come!

Liberty's full name was a family decision. We mulled over countless choices but Liberty constantly remained at the top of the list. The connotations were all correct. We wanted her to be independent but we also wanted her to have the grace and aestheticism of her breed. We wanted a feminine dog and the name Liberty leant itself to that image as well. It could mean the Statue of Liberty, turn of the century 'Liberty' style, Liberty fabric or Liberty, Equality, Fraternity. It seemed an ideal name, until she became a Bert.

Her other names were symbolic but less important. We acquired her on the first day of the Los Angeles Olympics, which determined her second name, and I stopped that day on the way to her kennels to buy some flowers, which precipitated her third name, Sweetpea. My youngest daughter had wanted to name the pup after a flower and this was her choice. The dog's final name had a self-evident source and at least it was better than a neighbour's dog who has had to live his life named Puddles.

Patrick Payence, a colleague who practises in Paris, has analysed the names that his clients give to their pets and again it is interesting that the majority give their pets human names like Victor and Sophie. Twenty-five per cent of his clients still give their pets animal names like Minou. Animal names such as Rover, Spot and Lassie are on the wane in England simply because as life gets more hectic pets are playing a more involved role in families. That role is difficult to explain but in part involves our need to escape, or at least to have breaks from the increasing pressures and tensions of a crowded and competitive urban life. And as our world has become more hectic we have looked upon our pets, bred them and named them, to satisfy our anthropomorphic needs. Sometimes however this goes too far.

In the 1970s I frequently used to see a well-known politician, an aggressive law and order man, and his pet gun dog. Whenever he talked to his dog he lapsed into babytalk, and on the odd occasion when he had to leave his dog with me for the day his regression into this childlike behaviour was actually embarrassing.

Regression is important in all of us because the child in us contributes to our charm and helps our creativity, but with this man, this outwardly tough guy, I couldn't help but feel that deep down inside he needed someone to hug but was afraid of showing his feelings to another person, so his dog, his non- judgemental gun dog, was the recipient of his feelings. This is pretty easy to do because most people see a smaller emotional distance between themselves and their pets than between themselves and other people.

As I have said, the child in us is in many ways our most valuable part and contributes pleasure to our family life. Breeding dogs to perpetuate childlike qualities, spontaneity, intuitiveness and a carefree nature, adds to the great pleasure that they give us. It also helps us because through our pets we can, at least for a little while, return to a gentler and more natural way of life.

When Honey was younger I used to take her each lunchtime for her daily exercise in Hyde Park. Because she was so obedient, she walked unfettered, without a lead, for the short distance to the park. She stopped at each intersection, waited for the signal, then ran full tilt to the next intersection and waited for me. At the zebra crossing at Bayswater Road, her last obstacle, she would stamp her feet with excitement and give me a constant, yearning, pleading, expressive look until I told her to proceed. Then she would hare into the park and tumble and roll in a state of near oblivion.

Honey was quite convinced that those daily excursions were only for her benefit and she wasn't altogether wrong. But they were for me too. There are times when being an adult is just no fun. Polite talk. Use of the grey matter. Responsibility. All these things can become oppressive sometimes. The benefits of civilisation don't help either. Traffic noise. Telephones. Bustle. Pet owners. Those daily walks with Honey, though, always brought a feeling of contentment. Sure, it wasn't the same as a paddle at dawn on a mirror-smooth mist-covered lake, but it was still an escape even if I was still in the heart of London, and what made it so was that dog's sniffing and investigating and rolling on worm mounds, meeting with circumspection other dogs and dashing headstrong for the Serpentine to pretend she was a submarine. Robert Benchley said, 'There is no doubt that every healthy, normal boy should own a dog at some time in his life, preferably between the ages of forty-five and fifty.' The humorist was a clever psychologist. The symbolic childlike behaviour of my dog is what gave me so much pleasure.

This is something that pet owners innately understand and is also why we breed animals and name them the way we do. We're using them for our own purposes. The lady who tried to register her dog's name as Sir O'Gate with the Kennel Club was simply being totally honest about the role she wanted her dog to fulfil. 'I'm forty and barren and honest,' she said to me. So was the divorced businesswoman who named her new dog Partner.

A psychiatrist friend once told me of a woman she knew who had nine budgies all named Gladys. That was done so that if any of them died she would still always have Gladys. A sensible woman! A client of mine has two dogs named Archie and Algie, but the dogs are also trained to respond to the names Killer and Prince and he uses the appropriate names in the appropriate circumstances. A sensible man!

Another client renames his cat after major people, places or events in his life. The cat started her life with the unlikely name of Disraeli but was soon renamed Pookie after a character in a film, a film that obviously had great significance for him. A year later the cat was renamed Aspen after the town in Colorado. Aspen's owner and his wife had had a marvellous skiing holiday there. Last year the cat was renamed Veronica and this year when I sent the owners a routine vaccination reminder he asked me to amend his record. He was now the sole owner of the cat. There was probably a fascinating story about a jealousy game there for the asking, but I didn't have the fortitude to ask.

4. JEALOUSY GAMES

PET: 'PAY ATTENTION *TO ME*'

All dogs will play jealousy games because the games are an integral part of normal canine dominance and submission behaviour. They will play jealousy games either with other dogs or with us for reasons of rivalry, because of their innate possessiveness or because of sex.

Samantha, a medium-sized mongrel of indeterminate lineage, is crazy about lovemaking. Not her own lovemaking, her owners'. Each time her owners get affectionate Samantha is, in a flash, on to the bed and muzzling her head around them. She worms her way around their necks, she breathes heavily in their ears (and gives the odd lick there too) and she tries to get between them. Samantha's lady owner says that there is glee in her dog's eyes when she gets on that bed – that she is almost smiling.

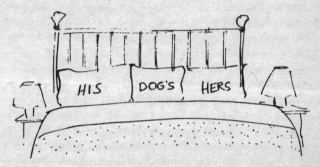

Samantha isn't unique. Sixty-five per cent of pet owners have reported that their pets try to 'muzzle in' when family members are affectionate to each other. These dogs either come to be petted, demand attention, wedge themselves between the people who are being affectionate or simply to join in. Their jealousy isn't restricted to lovemaking either. The simplest form of affection, even verbal affection, can provoke a jealous response from a pet, but interference in the nuptial bliss of a marriage can be one of the most exasperating manifestations. Years ago, a famous actor who had just married a much younger bride asked me if I could do something with their pet dog who positioned himself on the actor's shoulders each time he made love to his wife. It was a difficult problem made more so because of his wife's feeling of attachment for the dog.

Sex is, in fact, one of the lesser reasons for jealous behaviour in dogs. Possessiveness is far more important. Dogs that interfere when others show affection simply feel threatened. They see others getting 'stroked', getting attention and recognition, and join in for fear of being left out. Our dog Liberty is a typical example. She tries to muzzle in whenever any greeting is going on in the house; when the children come home from school, when visitors arrive, or when cuddles or squeezes are being provided. Her reaction, her 'my desires come first' type of behaviour, is natural with dogs, and because we knew it was natural it was possible to train her when she was a pup in such a way that we could reduce her natural possessive and jealous tendencies.

Most dogs enjoy having their own possessions and can be jealous or possessive if either a person or another dog tries to interfere with them. Retrievers in particular enjoy carrying their possessions, their tennis balls, rawhide chews and rubber rings, and parading them in front of people. The Retriever, because of its breeding to find shot birds and gently bring them back and relinquish them to its master rather than eat them, has a low jealousy rating when it comes to possessions (but a higher one when it comes to affection) and is one of the easiest breeds to train to 'drop it'.

When Liberty was a pup, whenever she possessively paraded one of her possessions in front of us she was trained to release the object on the command 'Drop it' and while she watched we would examine it, reward her with kind words or a stroke, then give it back to her. Similarly, when she tried to muzzle in for affection when the kids came home from school, when she tried to displace them, she was disregarded and only rewarded with affection once she had ceased interfering. The result is that she willingly gives up her treasures when asked to do so and now only greets people coming to the house rather then saying, 'Pay attention *to me*' to us when we greet visitors. Her jealousy level is low.

Terriers, on the other hand, haven't been bred for such low jealousy levels. Although they will drop on command and revel in playing fetch games, their possessiveness is such that they will play forever if given a chance to. What they are really doing, however, is saying, 'Pay attention *to me*'. James Thurber said, 'A hundred terriers have made me miserable since before the First World War by laying a ball at my feet and standing there panting and gasping and drooling until I throw it. Nobody my age can throw a baseball as far as I can, because of these years of practice. I am told that one Short-haired Fox Terrier, for whom I threw a ball all one afternoon, never did come back when I finally wound up and let go. Goody.'

Sex and possessiveness are two reasons for jealous behaviour in dogs and rivalry is the third; rivalry with other people and rivalry with other dogs. Recently a Cairn Terrier, one of two male littermates owned by the same family, was left with me for the day for a little minor dental surgery. Matthew and Horace went everywhere together and in fact were walked on the same single lead with two clips, one for each of their collars. Their owner told me that, when Matthew was left with me, Horace positively bounced out of the clinic and floated down the street. And when he got home he raced around the house throwing his toys in the air *and throwing Matthew's toys in the air*. He had temporarily been freed from the rivalry with his brother.

In most instances the owner is the focus for rivalry and jealousy games are played out to get the owner's attention and to get 'strokes', recognition, from the owner.

Matthew and Horace have been fighting at home since they were around ten months old but their fights have always only occurred in one situation, and that is when one of the dogs is allowed on their owner's lap. When that happens the other will suffer a positive avalanche of rage. He will show his teeth, snarl, growl, and he will carry a grudge. Once the other is off the owner's lap, even if it is hours later, it will be attacked. They fight mercilessly and because they are so equal there is never a clear winner. (Maybe I am the winner. I keep being

called upon to repair the dogs.) Both dogs are playing a straightforward rivalry game for their leader's attention. Their jealousy of each other exists only to say in a way that each instinctively knows best, 'Pay attention *to me*'.

Most pet owners try to be even-handed with their pets, to treat them equally and democratically so that there will be no possible reason for jealousy. They forget that in the canine world there is little call for democracy and when jealousy exists the owner has to decide which animal will be dominant. This goes against the philosophy of most pet owners. 'I can't do that to him,' they tell me when I describe how the owner must always greet one dog first, feed it first, allow only that dog on furniture or laps, put its lead on first. Horace and Matthew's owners have never had the strength to do it. Nevertheless, if you want to have any effect on stopping jealousy games between dogs you have to decide which dog will be dominant.

Once you do, you reinforce that dominance in the ways I've mentioned and then proceed to discipline them for misbehaviour as I have outlined under the treatment for 'Simon says . . .' games (p. 114). If both dogs are male and jealous fighting is severe, it is sometimes necessary to castrate one or treat one with hormones so that the dominance–submission difference between the two is greater.

A very special and very difficult form of jealousy can occur in families where the pet is the first 'child' and a real baby is the second. In this situation some pets can show intense jealousy and in my mind if there is even the hint of possible danger to the baby the pet should be rehomed. If the pet has big teeth and has a known jealous disposition it isn't worth the risk of trying to modify its behaviour.

There are certain rules to follow when introducing a baby into a home already occupied by a pet. These rules apply equally to the introduction of a new pup or kit to the home. First of all, don't alter your pet's existing routine. Dogs and cats are creatures of habit and don't take kindly to changes. Exercise them, feed them and play with them as you always have done.

Introduce your pet to the smells of the new baby: a soiled nappy, powders, foods. Let your pet investigate the new things in your house and let it have a good sniff around the baby's room.

Both babies and pups and kits should be introduced to the resident pet while the little ones are sleeping. And always reinforce your pet's good behaviour by rewarding it with petting or food. Dogs might be jealous of new pups for a short while but a dog's need to be sociable is almost irresistible and sooner or later, usually in less than three weeks, all the initial jealousy will be gone.

Cats are different. A cat that has had a home to itself and has never lived with other cats will probably be jealous of any new cat that enters its abode and that jealousy may *never* disappear. Cats don't necessarily need other feline companions in the way dogs need canine compatriots.

Remember, let inquisitive dogs investigate. It will reduce any possible jealousy problems that you might encounter. Pay as much attention to your dog as you always have so that he or

she will not have to play 'Pay attention *to me*' with you. The
jealousy that a dog feels is a simple jealousy and its treatment
is usually obvious. The jealousy that owners feel is much
more complicated and emotionally of more significance and
consequence.

OWNER: 'YOU LOVE THAT ANIMAL MORE THAN YOU LOVE ME'

She hated the budgie. She was a graduate psychologist and
knew exactly what was happening but she still hated the bird
with a passion, with real venom. Her husband didn't know
that he was displacing his affection on to the budgie, that he
was singing to it and not to his wife, but his wife did. Her
post-graduate training should have overcome her feelings but
it didn't. She only felt jealousy and anger. She had malicious
daydreams – barbecued budgie, southern fried budgie, budgie
à l'orange, budgie soup. She dreamed of presenting the budgie
to her husband at the dinner table, surrounded by roast
potatoes and with a flag in its cooked pectorals – 'Mickey –
RIP'.

Her jealousy of this hundred grams of blue feathers was
displaced anger just as much as her husband's crooning to the
bird was displaced affection.

As I see it, if there is jealousy of a household pet there is a
major problem somewhere but it is judgemental on my part to
say where the problem lies.

One of the reasons that a pet owner can transfer his or her
affection to a pet in the first place is because the pet is non-
judgemental. Pets don't judge owners. They simply offer what
we interpret as loyalty. They are constant children, always
subordinate in a parent–child manner, and they never
change. It means that in a funny sort of way they are easier to
get to know than people are because their personalities and
behaviour are constant and unchanging.

People's personalities are constantly evolving but a dog's or
cat's temperament remains pretty constant throughout its life.

The pet's personality is familiar and solid. This leads to a certain type of intimacy that some pet owners have with their pets – a warmth and a closeness that comes from familiarity. Eye to eye contact can be easy between a person and his pet and this intensifies the relationship. The type of touching and talking that exists in a good person–pet relationship also intensifies the feeling of relaxation and warmth that some people can have with their animals. All of these are reasons why some people might find it easier to be intimate with their pets than with other people.

Joanna and John knew that their cat was dying and that's why both of them had brought Sylvester in. Sylvester had leukemia and through mutual consent we had decided that the end should come now. I hadn't met John before. As with the majority of cases, I had only met his wife whenever Sylvester needed veterinary treatment. Even in an area of London where many women work, it still seems that it is the woman's responsibility to take the pets to the vet's.

I had spoken to John on the telephone just after there had been confirmation that Sylvester had leukemia. He wanted to know if there was any treatment and I had explained that with a certain combination of drugs and radiation therapy, the disease could sometimes be overcome. We had discussed the possible treatment at length but because of the cat's age, the uncertainty of success and the investment in time that would be involved, he and his wife opted for a palliative treatment instead and now that this was no longer having the desired effect they were with me for my final intervention.

They both wanted to stay while I injected Sylvester and they both stayed afterwards too. Joanna seemed to keep a stiff upper lip but John couldn't control his sorrow and he sobbed and sobbed and buried his hand in the fur of the emaciated body of his pet. After this had gone on for a couple of minutes Joanna asked John, 'Are you going to cry for me so hard when I die?' He didn't answer but I felt surprised and uncomfortable by her question. It just didn't seem to be the time or the place to show or to feel such jealousy. The cat was dead!

If he's so smart, how come he picked you?

Joanna's jealousy might simply be there because although she is attractive and apparently self-confident and controlled she might, underneath it all, be a gargantuan mass of insecurities. She might have a mammoth inferiority complex under her smooth exterior. Otherwise why would she try to make her husband feel guilty at such a heart-breaking time? I don't know. That's a question for the psychologists to answer. What I do know is that I see pet owners play 'You love that animal more than you love me' and I know that on one side of the equation or other there are serious problems.

People can make great emotional investments in their pets. If the investment is open and accepted with honesty from both sides of the marriage, the investment will be constructive and will almost undoubtedly pay dividends. Pets can and should enhance marriages.

But if there are problems already existing in a marriage, a pet can make these problems proportionately greater. The pet can become a focus for conflict. If the pet is used to displace the normal giving and taking of love and affection then the owners of that pet are probably just storing up problems for themselves. The pet is probably storing up problems for itself too and I will discuss this in the next chapter under Scapegoat Games.

CHAPTER SIX

Displacement Games

1. DESTRUCTION GAMES

PET: 'JUST CALL ME ATTILA'

They knew they had been vandalised as soon as they opened their front door but they didn't know that the vandal was still there. A table lamp was lying on the floor. Their favourite Wedgwood Fairyland lustre bowl lay smashed to pieces. And their old Beluchi Persian carpet from the hallway, the one they treasured most, was gone – stolen!

At least Bruno was OK. Bruno, their fourteen-month-old St Bernard, gave them his usual glorious greeting when they arrived. He wagged himself silly and jumped up on his male owner to lick his face in a typical canine greeting. 'A fine watch dog,' they said to each other as they catalogued the damage. Bruno was there, in no small part, to protect the house. The Johnsons, his owners, live in a part of London that is called 'up and coming'. It hasn't been gentrified yet and their risk of burglary is proportionally high. They were the first couple to buy a dilapidated house on their run-down street and to repair it; to strip the front door down to natural wood, to reinstate the brass fittings, to restore the stained-glass window, to renew the tiles in the fireplace, to install central heating – 'Chelsify' as they say in London. And they knew that until the rest of the area was 'Chelsified' they stood out like a ripe fat thumb and ran a high risk of being hit by burglars.

That was why they got such a big dog. Bruno was there to scare away intruders and now, when the awful event had finally happened, it turned out that he had done nothing. The Johnsons were, in fact, a little relieved that he had done nothing because at least he was unharmed. As with most pet owners they had developed a strong bond with Bruno in the year they had had him and by now his wellbeing was more important than the safety of their inanimate possessions.

The Johnsons went from room to room itemising what was damaged or lost and were grateful to find nothing else out of place, but when they got to the bedroom they stared in disbelief. Their bed was in a shambles. The bedspread, blankets and sheets had been ruthlessly stripped away and some seemingly superhuman force had rent a ragged hole in the middle of the mattress. And in that hole was the remains of their Beluchi carpet – shredded! *Bruno was the vandal!*

Bruno continued to wag his tail deliciously and to smile his greetings. He showed no guilt. He showed no remorse. He showed no brains either because as the Johnsons looked on slack-jawed, he leapt on to the bed and barked joyously to them.

Bruno's behaviour was perhaps an inevitability – a young giant left at home alone all day and most evenings because both of his owners worked, given a postage-stamp-sized back garden to exercise in and no stimulation or activity other than the occasional walk; bought for security duty with no thought given to the animal's needs.

The Johnsons aren't the only couple who have made that type of mistake. In the last five years, the five breeds that have grown fastest in popularity in Britain are the Rottweiler, Dobermann, Staffordshire Bull Terrier, German Shepherd and Boxer – all 'defence' dogs and all needing bounteous exercise. There are tens of thousands of dogs in this country that sit in their luxury jails, ostensibly protecting their homes but in fact deprived of almost all forms of normal stimulation. (It's interesting that the breeds that are fastest growing in popularity in the United States are quite different. They are the Cocker Spaniel, Golden Retriever, Shetland Sheepdog, Basset Hound and Yorkshire Terrier. Their ability to wreak havoc in a house is probably as great as the British list but they certainly couldn't be classified as large defence breeds.)

Bruno's problem was dead simple to diagnose. He was simply frustrated at being left at home alone and he vented his frustrations on objects in the house. He 'displaced' his frustrations by damaging things.

I've already mentioned under Manipulation Games how dogs and cats can express their exasperation or anxiety by leaving solid or liquid gifts for their owners, another form of displacement activity. Destructive activities such as chewing Persian carpets, jumping up on people, digging holes in the garden (or in mattresses), excessive barking or even chewing themselves, especially their front legs, are all displacement games where the animals show their distress by being destructive.

I hate to use my dog Liberty as a negative example again. She really is a well-mannered dog, sort of. But I will.

Chewing is a natural activity for a dog and all pups should be given a specific toy to chew. They should be taught as pups that certain things are 'chewable' and others are not. In Liberty's case we gave her a rubber ring and a rawhide chew. If you give a dog too many toys you will be impeding its training because the dog will not understand that its chewing activity should be restricted. If it's allowed to chew ten different toys it will probably chew other things as well whereas if it is only allowed to chew, at most, three objects, the training can be more effective.

Honey used to greet us at the door by racing up to the bedroom and returning with one of my sheepskin slippers in her mouth and then parading in front of us with it, so we thought it was cute when Liberty as a pup first picked up one of the children's similar slippers. I didn't think it was so funny later when she was older when she turned one of mine inside out and left it plucked.

A pup's unwanted chewing behaviour can be simply corrected just by saying 'no' when the pup chews something unacceptable and by replacing it with one of the pup's toys, acceptable chewthings.

If a mature dog is chewing things (or digging up the garden or constantly jumping up on people for that matter) then that is a different matter.

Getting angry probably helps. It certainly helps *you* and if you show the dog the damage it may, it just may understand your displeasure. These destruction games most likely occur in the owner's absence and it is important to understand that a dog doesn't tear up carpet because it hates the pattern or chew a wall because it's sick of Laura Ashley prints. It does these things because it is bored and frustrated and is displacing its need for activity into the wrong channels.

The solution, of course, is to change the dog's lifestyle so that it is no longer bored and no longer has the need to burn up energy in frustrating pursuits. This is in most instances, however, an unrealistic approach. People can't quit their jobs to exercise their dogs. What it means then is that the dog's frustrations have to be cooled, and channelled into less destructive activity. If you have a grown-up vandal, a 'Just call me Attila' type of dog, then this is what you should do.

'People can't quit their jobs to exercise their dogs'

1. Withdraw all affection-giving to the dog. From now on it has to earn it.
2. Reintroduce obedience training until your dog obeys 'come', 'sit' and 'stay'.
3. If your dog is consistently chewing one thing, make that thing as unpleasant as possible. Although most dogs seem

to lose their taste discrimination and will chew anything if they're really frustrated, use one of the sprays or paints marketed for inhibiting kids from chewing their nails. (My colleague in Toronto, Paul McCutcheon, advises his clients that if they have cats that chew the houseplants to set mousetraps under thin paper around the plant pots. When the cat steps on the paper the trap springs. He says this type of aversion therapy works a treat and besides, you find out what the cat was up to when you return home.)

4. Avoid doing things by which your dog will associate you with discipline. The monks of New Skete in their excellent book on dog training advise pet owners to 'use magic'. The magic I advise the owners of the Attilas of dogdom to employ is a high-velocity water pistol. A well-aimed blast when a grown-up cat or dog is chewing or scratching (or peeing for that matter – appropriate aversion therapy for that problem!) can work wonders. Remember that as well as magic, dogs are susceptible to habit, routine, leadership, praise and rewards.

5. Give the dog one or two acceptable chewthings. It's even acceptable to play tug-of-war with these things to reinforce the fun that they give. Liberty has a rubber ring and a series of tennis balls. The disadvantage of the rubber ring is that young dogs like Liberty might develop their own private 'fetch' games as she has. She's thrown her ring into the fireplace (and on to the fire), on to the dining-room table, over the back of the sofa and against the window. It comes winging through the air like a guided missile. In her mouth it's a weapon.

6. Praise your dog for chewing its chewthing. Discipline him for chewing anything else.

Now you are ready to train him to give up his destructive ways when you are away from home.

1. Think seriously about getting your dog a companion – another dog, a cat, even a singing bird. Liberty can sit quizzically for minutes at a time looking at my African grey parrot Humphrette. If that is out of the question leave a TV or a radio on when you leave him alone all day.

2. Leave the house quietly and return calmly. Don't be edgy or dramatic because your dog will pick up the signals. Bursting in at the end of the day with treats and cuddles might alleviate your guilt (of which more will be said shortly) but it's of no value for your dog.

3. Take your dog's chewthing away from him a couple of hours before you go out then handle it well just before you give it back to him, just before you leave. This will leave your scent on it.

4. Go through a mock departure. Put on your coat, pick up your briefcase, do whatever you normally do when you leave but only leave for five to ten minutes.

5. If your dog has been good (no destructive games – no chewing, no barking, no self-mutilation) gently reward him for his good behaviour when you return. Give him a treat, take him for a little exercise, give him some 'strokes', signs of recognition.

6. If your dog has been destructive, reprimand him and isolate and ignore him for a short while.

7. Continue playing fun games with the dog (and his chewthing) each day to reinforce in his mind the enjoyment of that object. Give him as much vigorous exercise as possible.

8. Vary your schedule of departures each day. Dogs are creatures of habit and if you leave for exactly fifteen minutes each and every day during your retraining you may end up with a dog that learns to wait to the sixteenth minute before being destructive. Leave for, say, twenty minutes the next day, then 15, 30, 20, 40 and 25 minutes on subsequent days.

With perseverance you should be able to train all but the most delinquent of pets to reduce their destructive activity. One after-effect, however, is that if you have a dog or cat that is frustrated and bored and destructive because of its isolation, and if you are a good and sensitive owner, you will feel guilty.

Owner: 'He Did It to Get Even'

Guilt is the natural reaction of good pet owners when they discover that their pet's destructive activity is caused by frustration and boredom. But it can be an erroneous reaction too.

One of my clients has two cats, one an elegant-looking Persian, and she wrote this to me.

> My Persian, Mr Daisy, is very jealous, not of Muffin who was here when I first got him as a kitten but of the other strays I have looked after. *He punishes me* [my italics] by spraying all over the place, which I find very exhausting to clean or to wash over and over again. I try to show him even more love but he won't stop. He is a beast to the two females. He sits guard so they can't go to the litter box and when Poppy (she is one of the strays) wants to go she runs about my bedroom on and off my bed which is her way of telling me she has to go and I have to bring her downstairs, wait for her and bring her back.

The owner's analysis of the situation is quite right except for one detail. Mr Daisy isn't punishing her. That's just her guilt. He's spraying because he's distressed by the presence of strange cats on his territory.

The lady's feeling that Mr Daisy 'did it to get even' is a common reaction. Lots of my clients tell me that their pets have done nasty things to get back at them for just taking the pet on a visit to see me! Guilt can be pointless. A dog that misbehaves, that barks, chews or destroys, has to be disciplined and owners should be firm enough to do so. They should also be big enough to make up but not so guilt-ridden that they over make up. Too much coddling and cuddling, sympathising and rewarding, is pointless. Folks sometimes ask me for tranquillisers for their dogs because the animals have to be left alone all day. Tranquillisers are fine for single-event problems like fright from fireworks noise, but wanting to give tranquillisers to a dog five days a week is simply overcompensating for the guilt the owner feels for leaving the animal alone at home all day.

The cat is fine, the tablets are for your pet complex

Instead of investing energy in guilt pet owners should invest that energy in redirecting their pet's need for activity into more constructive channels and if this is done properly it can result in good wholesome family entertainment.

Sherpa, a Lhasa Apso, has been taught a simple game that keeps both the dog and his family amused. It's also an excuse for the whole family to still do something together. Sherpa has a few favourite toys and he is invited into the living room by his owners and their children and is shown one of them. He's then told to go out into the hall and count to ten. While he's out there (counting) his family hides the toy. Sherpa is then told he can come back into the room and he plays 'Treasure Hunt'. When he moves away from the hidden toy they all say 'colder' and when he moves closer to it they all say 'warmer'. When he gets real close they shout 'hot' and Sherpa gets really excited and when he finds it they all applaud. Then he sits down and they show him the next object they are going to hide and on his own he goes back out into the hall, sits down and starts counting to ten again. It provides activity for the dog and reduces any guilt that the owners might have for not paying enough attention to him during the day.

There are lots of other games that you can teach dogs, games that complement the dog's own specific needs. Breeds like Retrievers should be taught 'fetch' games. They should carry newspapers or small parcels home each day. Dogs that have a greater need to vent their frustrations through barking should be taught to 'alarm bark'. They should be inhibited from barking except under certain circumstances. It's not difficult to do. First of all train the dog to bark to the word 'speak' by rewarding it with food or affection when it does so. Later it should bark when you ask it to 'speak'. It's a sensible game to teach for two reasons. The first is that each time you exercise the dog you can play the game. That will be a release for the dog and also continual reinforcement of the training. The second is that, especially if the dog can look the part of a protector or defender and if you live in an area where a defender might come in handy, it can be helpful to have a good bluffer around.

Parlour tricks are also good for both you and your dog. Old Honey's favourite parlour trick was a good one. She used to take visitors' wedding rings off their fingers with a delicacy that was so exquisite you'd swear she could thread a needle if given the opportunity. Her only misfortune occurred one day when, after she had taken my wife's wedding ring off and while she was parading with it in her mouth, a friend gave her a hefty wallop on her side to tell her how well she had done and I ended up inducing the ring back by means of an injection in her front leg.

Positive activities, training, parlour tricks and games should involve the whole family and should be approached with relish, gusto and vigour. If they are fun for you as well as the dog they will go a great way towards diminishing the guilty feelings you might have about the lifestyle you impose on your pet. And if they are good games they might develop into rituals, something I shall discuss next.

2. RITUAL AND GIFT GAMES

Pet: 'Don't Ask Me Why I Do It, I Just Do It'

Carol Gould's cat Mango is a rubber fetishist. The owner says, 'Every night from the very first day I adopted her [she was eight weeks old then] she has placed my rubber gloves for washing up by the door which separates the sitting room and the foyer leading to my bedroom. She sleeps in the sitting room and I sleep in the bedroom, and she performs this "rubber glove ritual" every night! Not that it annoys me – I find it an adorable eccentricity – but could you unravel the mystery behind this curious behaviour?'

Well, I couldn't and I still can't, but I can give a few rational explanations for some of the more obvious rituals that pets perform.

Dogs are like children in that they love routine and ritual. (They are also like kids in that they enjoy surprises as long as they are involved in them.) Dogs like rituals because they use them to maintain their places in the social order, and by doing that they get 'stroked'; they get social recognition. Hunting, feeding, greeting and sleeping rituals are all performed in order for the dog to get social recognition.

Sleeping rituals are amongst the most common. Nobody

has yet come up with a confirmed explanation of why dogs ritually turn before they lie down (I think it's simply to get all the appendages in the right place) but there is a simple and logical reason for their apparent ritual desire to sleep in their owners' bedrooms. Obviously they want the security of the presence of other members of their packs. Dogs are, as we know, intensely social animals and they crave companionship, but there are other reasons too.

As far as dogs are concerned, there are two favourite places in the house, the kitchen and the bedroom. Rewards in the kitchen are only intermittent but rewards in the bedroom are continuous. The bedroom can provide constant exhilaration. After all, it smells of socks and underwear and sex and all sorts of things that tickle the tastebuds. The bedroom is an odorific delight! It smells of the pack. You and I may not notice it but dogs and cats with their exquisitely sensitive senses of smell can.

That's one of the reasons why some dogs have gift rituals too – a greeting at the door with an overripe sock, or the presentation of a pair of knickers to welcome the visitors. When dogs bring gifts like that they are simply reinforcing their status in their packs. There are, however, other gift rituals that are played out for different reasons.

My brother has visitors to his home on most week nights. My brother is a florist and the visitors are there to discuss the flowers for their wedding and one of the first trials they have to pass is the 'Whisky test'. Whisky is a female black whippet-like mongrel with an overdeveloped gift-giving talent. All visitors are brought gifts and my brother marks them on their ability or inclination to respond. Whisky brings gifts until she is acknowledged – until she is 'stroked'. Once that is done she feels secure because her social status has been confirmed, but if the visitor does not 'stroke' her she remains perplexed and continues to strive for recognition. Her record to date is twenty-seven unacknowledged gifts! By the time that bride had left, Whisky had created a mountain in the living room

He's a lousy owner but he's got great socks

that had started with balls and bones, worked its way through
socks and shoes and had finished with the blanket off their
bed. My brother was convinced that if that bride hadn't left
when she did Whisky would have dragged the fridge in next.
(He also had to be convinced by his wife not to make that
bride's bouquet out of dead flowers. Love me – love my dog!)

Cats will carry out their gift rituals in a more natural
manner – more natural in that given the opportunity their
gifts will be mice, birds and birds' eggs. Their reasoning will
still be the same, social recognition. Cats don't have quite as
many greeting rituals as dogs do and certainly don't strive as
hard as Whisky did for recognition, but there is at least one
cat in London with its own unique way of saying hello. If you
telephone his owners and they are not at home, he knocks the
receiver off the phone and on to the floor then settles himself
down and purrs into it.

Feeding rituals can be instinctive or they can be learned.
When Liberty was a pup she was taken to meet my sister-in-

I knew she'd like it

law's Bearded Collie, Willow. My wife described their first meeting this way. 'Libby didn't know exactly what to do and she bit Willow too hard and Willow told her off. Libby said she was sorry but she did it again and then Willow sulked, so Libby sat on her head and that made Willow play again. Then they were friends again and Willow taught Libby how to stand in her water bowl while drinking.'

Liberty still does stand in her bowl if allowed to. She also quizzically tries to catch the drops that fall back from her face. She sees them hit the surface of the water and with her muzzle she dives to the bottom of her bowl looking for them. She digs underneath in case they've escaped through the bottom. My dog may be a clown but she has no dignity.

Gerald, a Labrador, has a feeding ritual that is instinctive rather than learned. Most members of the canine family will bury food and then come back to it later to eat it. That's of course why dogs bury bones. The three Yorkshire Terriers I grew up with used to bury their Bonios in the garden my father had built in our living room. We'd find the biscuits planted there like crosses in a war cemetery. Each evening Gerald goes to the cupboard and takes out a can of Chum dog food. Then he goes outside and he buries it. His owners calculate that at any given time he probably has at least a month's supply in reserve. The nuisance with his ritual is that he is only partly fulfilling his instinctive urges because he never seems to remember where he has buried the goodies.

Hunting rituals are also instinctive. Singing dogs sing to call the pack. Only today in an urban dog the stimulus to sing might be a Kiri Te Kanawa record. Terriers and other breeds ritually shake boxes of Kleenex or torn rags to death because deep down inside, deep in their primitive cores, they'd really like to do it to a rat or some other creature. One of my clients had told me of a huge Siamese cat he once owned when he lived in the west of Ireland thirty years ago. The cat, Tripi, used to go rabbit hunting with him; he'd have his gun on one shoulder and his cat on the other. The cat would also hunt on his own but his hunting had become ritualised in a modified way, in that he hunted the wrong prey. He hunted cows. 'Tripi would lie on the branch of an oak tree which hung over the track up to the farm, and when the cows used to go up there in the evening he would fall on their necks. He could never understand why they could just shake him off. We often saw him stalking them in the fields too.'

Elimination rituals are either learned or instinctive. Some dogs will instinctively kick up some earth (or pavement if they are city dwellers) to mark their droppings. Droppings, as we know, are territory markers. Other dogs will develop rituals through experience. When Liberty was a pup she was trained to use the gutter on the road beside the house. That was in the summer and the road was always bumper to bumper with cars . she usually found herself squatting under a bumper. Now that she is full grown she often ritually searches out a car, crouches down to get her head under the bumper (and this usually means putting one forepaw up on the pavement for balance) and in this contorted position empties her bladder. It's a learned ritual behaviour.

My nurse's dog, Tessa, is even worse. She will only urinate on plastic bags, although no one in her family seems to know why. And Maxine is so desensitised to the idiosyncracy that she sometimes finds herself stuffing a plastic bag in her pocket before she takes her grouchy old Labrador-like beast for a walk.

Perhaps the most ingrained rituals that pets perform are those that are based on their biological clocks. Dogs have amazing biological clocks and once they are trained into certain habits, they can calculate almost to the minute their hour to hour activities and carry out behaviour rituals so that their routine is not altered. They do that because as long as their routine is not altered their social position remains secure.

Honey used to stand each day at noon at my examining-room door, looking expectantly at me. It didn't matter whether she was in the deepest sleep at 11.55, at noon she was ritually at the door and she was there because she knew that if I was going on house visits that's when I'd be leaving and that was her chance to go for a ride in the car (and hopefully end up in the park).

When she was older her biological clock caused her to indulge in more ritual behaviour. Honey would spend all evening with the family in the living room and at 11 o'clock she would get up and saunter upstairs to her basket. But at midnight, if Julia and I hadn't gone to bed yet, she was back down. 'It's midnight. You're always in bed by midnight,' she said with her behaviour. 'Why aren't you in bed?'

With time, a dog's play activity becomes ritualised too. Some dogs will exercise only with a ball in the month. Bejo, my parents' 'Dubai Terrier', finishes each play activity with a ritualised growl and attack. Liberty now ritually throws her rubber ring behind the sofa and then digs, involving us in getting it back for her.

Shortly after I put down a very elderly collie-type dog, his owner, scarcely older than the dog, wrote to me about him. In her letter she said,

> He started to play football from the age of six weeks old. He was never trained to do it. It was just a natural thing to him. He actually used to kick the ball with his paw but he always had to have a tin can in his mouth. Why I don't know. It sounds funny but he would never play football unless he had a tin can in his mouth.
>
> He always played at the Whitfield Public Gardens. He was loved by many people in the Goodge Street and Tottenham Court Road area. As people passed the gardens to go about their business they always stopped to watch him. He never failed to have an audience.

well Brian, I feel as sick
as a poodle - I mean parrot

He would play on his own for hours but when he got bored he would look around at the people sitting on the wooden benches in the public gardens and he would kick the ball with his paw under the bench of someone sitting there. Then he would stand in front of that person looking at him straight in the eyes until that person realised that the dog wanted him to throw the ball. Then the dog would kick it back to him. When he got fed up with that person he would move on to another bench. He was known as 'the dog that plays football'. He played up to the age of fourteen years old and although he still loved playing with the ball he hadn't got the strength any more.

Her description of her old friend was a poignant one because she was saying something about herself too. In telling me these things she was telling me how important that dog was to her. The ritual games we play through our pets are just as important as the ritual games they play with us.

OWNER: 'I'M A SILLY PUSSY'

Her cat was on the examining table simply because he'd been bitten on his backside again. Arnold was a bit of a coward and never seemed to have head to head confrontations with other cats. With him it was always head to bum and once more he was with me because of a simple abscess which had to be drained. Arnold's owner, however, was having near hysterics. 'He's going to die. I know he's going to die.' Nothing I could say could interrupt her self-satisfying worry and with the assistance of one of my nurses I quickly lanced the abscess, drained out the pus, flushed the wound, gave the cat an injection of long-acting antibiotics and handed Arnold back to his owner.

'Take him home and I'm sure that by this evening his appetite will be back,' I said and Arnold's owner looked at me and replied, 'He's going to get better? Oh I *am* a silly pussy.' She left and we amused ourselves with her self-description but her act of ritual identification with her cat was not all that unusual.

Not long afterwards a man came in with his mature male cat. The cat's problem, he said, was that it had lost its appetite and was restless at night. He continued to explain that for the cat's entire life it had slept with his wife but she had died two weeks previously and he didn't think the cat understood and that was why it was restless and off its food. As the owner told me this I saw his eyes fill with tears but he was too proud to permit a single drop to flow down his cheek so I concurred with him in a remote, distant and dispassionate way; that his analysis of the situation was probably correct but that given time, a cat could cope with grief – it just needed time.

Pet owners may or may not know that they allow their pets to play ritual roles on their owner's behalf or for their owner's own satisfaction. A pet can ritually play the role of relative, protector, companion, or uncritical lover. Jilly Cooper once described her dog as a 'glorious delinquent', an unusual and revealing choice of words.

Pets can ritually be used to act as go-betweens in human relationships, to act as catalysts for us. They can also be seen as ritual care-givers. One person who wrote to me said this about her cat: 'Some months ago when I was taken very ill in the middle of the night Bogey sat up on his hind legs touching my face with his pawless leg and trying to comfort me. [I had had to previously amputate his paw.] Bogey was almost human in his behaviour and when my doctor arrived Bogey had to be pushed away. He was almost on top of me, protecting me, trying to help me.' In her mind Bogey was the ritual healer but in fact all that he was probably after was a little extra body heat. Cats love warmth and there's nothing finer than a human with a high fever for a cat to snuggle up to.

The ritual image of the cat is that of an independent, aristocratic, courageous, decorative, unrestrained and dignified being, equal to us or perhaps even superior. Not so the dog. The dog may be all of these things to some people but he is also ritually seen as a sycophant and is treated as such. That's why you can buy camouflage rainwear and bomber jackets for your dog and choose between crystal and onyx or grey flannel collars. Can you imagine a cat in a designer track suit or wearing its own personal life jacket, two items you can buy for your dog at Harrods in London? The manager of the pet department of Macy's in New York summed up the ritual role-playing approach to dogs quite nicely when he was asked whether his dog wore anything from his department. 'I've got a guard dog,' he was reported as saying. 'You put a peach satin baby-doll outfit on a big dog – well, it can look kind of sleazy.'

Pet owners may permit their pets to play out ritual activities but the owners are probably allowing the games for their own reasons. Otherwise how can you explain some owner behaviour? Talking about the same dog she described as a 'glorious delinquent', Jilly Cooper said, 'If people came to the house who he didn't like or who didn't like him, he ate their shoes.' Why let him? More common is the ritual biting that pet owners are willing to put up with. Why do they allow it? Some rituals have an obvious purpose. Mrs Green took her Beagle, Higgins, to Hyde Park each day of his life and each day she lost him. It was a ritual. The day would be spent looking for Higgins. Everyone knew Higgins and Mrs Green because she met all the park regulars on her daily quests for her lost canine. The ritual gave both him and his owner much more exercise than they would otherwise have got. They were park fixtures.

Some rituals are enforced by society. Bartok Lorenzen, a Cocker Spaniel, until recently had his own season ticket complete with full face photo for the London Underground, because it was required if he was to qualify for the cheapest transit rates.

Society indulges in more transparent rituals and nowhere more so than in law. Consider this report from *The Times*:

MIAOW COSTS YOUTH £100

Lawrence O'Dowd, aged 18 and unemployed, was fined £100 yesterday by York magistrates for saying 'miaow' to a police dog.

The youth was arrested by the dog's handler, Acting Sergeant Fred Taylor, and charged with using threatening and abusive words and behaviour likely to occasion a breach of the peace.

O'Dowd was also bound over in the sum of £100 to keep the peace for two years. He said afterwards, 'I can't believe it.'

The bench was told that O'Dowd miaowed at the dog Peel, after being ordered to move on by Sgt Taylor.

Mr Peter Gildener, for the prosecution, told the court that O'Dowd was one of a group of youngsters outside a shop one Saturday in September. The policeman approached because the youths were using bad language and blocking the footpath.

Sgt Taylor said that as he approached O'Dowd looked at him and miaowed. He considered the miaow abusive in the situation.'

The English courts are not alone in integrating animals into their rituals. Let me quote from the transcript of *Conti* v. *ASPCA*, a civil case from New York in which Mr Conti claimed that a parrot that he had found but that was now in the possession of the American Society for the Prevention of Cruelty of Animals, was really his. The ASPCA said it was theirs before he went missing.

The representatives of the defendent ASPCA were categorical in their testimony that the parrot was indeed Chester, that he was unique because of his size, color and habits. They claimed that Chester said 'hello' and could dangle by his legs. During the entire trial the court had the parrot under close scrutiny but at no time did it exhibit any of these characteristics. The court called upon the parrot to indicate by name or other mannerism an affinity to either of the claimed owners. Alas the parrot stood mute.

'Alas the parrot stood mute.' If nothing else the ritual certainly proves that there is still a sense of humour in the judicial system.

Pets play many roles for their owners. They can allow some people to express or even live out important or maybe unconscious aspects of themselves. But there is one evil ritual activity that some people will play with their pets and that is the scapegoat. I will get to that shortly.

3. SCAPEGOAT GAMES

Pet: 'I'll Stalk You, I'll Catch You, I'll Kill You'

The Shih Tzu was at death's door and if it hadn't been for my more experienced nurse I could have been Dr Death. It was my thirty-sixth day in practice, a quiet Saturday morning with just one nurse and myself on duty to see a few overflow cases from the preceding week. We were chatting in reception when the man rushed in with his limp rag of a pet in his hands.

From a distance the dog appeared simply lifeless but when I looked closer I saw that it was severely injured. Its chest had been torn open and one of its lungs was stuck on a broken rib. I reached for my stethoscope but my nurse, Pat, diplomatically suggested to me that we'd better get it to the operating room immediately and briskly but gently whisked the body away. I excused myself from the owner and went downstairs, by which time Pat had placed a tube down its windpipe and was 'bagging' it, breathing for it by squeezing pure oxygen from an oxygen cylinder through an inflated bag down the endotracheal tube and into its lungs. I listened with my stethoscope and heard the heart beating and while Pat continued to bag the dog, I got out the necessary sterile packs for surgery. Through her immediate actions she had genuinely saved the dog's life but now it was up to me to carry out the repairs. I didn't know it at the time but the Shih Tzu was a scapegoat, the victim of a displacement game perpetrated by a large German Shepherd.

Once Pat had got both the dog and me through the initial crisis I was confident in my abilities to correct the injuries. Although I had been in practice for only six weeks and had been quite useless when the dog was initially brought in, my surgical training at university was on a par with the best and in fact I had performed a lung operation similar to what was now needed as a surgical exercise during my clinical years. While Pat continued to bag the dog, now with a mixture of anaesthetic gas and oxygen, I removed the most damaged lung tissue, removed or repositioned the fractured ribs and sewed up the wounds. The Shih Tzu was a solid dog and she made an uneventful recovery, but her injuries puzzled me. Why had she been attacked in that manner?

Her owner described what had happened and his description eliminated many of the justifiable causes of aggression between dogs. He had been exercising his neutered two-year-old female Shih Tzu in Hyde Park that morning, as he always did, when he noticed at a distance a German Shepherd lying down but alertly watching his dog. Hyde Park often seems to have as many dogs in it taking their exercise as it has people and he was used to other dogs taking an interest in his dog. That was in fact why she had been spayed, but he was a little worried by the German Shepherd's behaviour.

As his dog sniffed and smelled and carried out her ablutions the Shepherd edged nearer, crawling along the ground, never getting off its belly. It was apparently oblivious to the other dogs and people in the park and seemed to concentrate with a laser-like intensity on his small bundle of beige and white fur as she continued to meander around, unaware of the eyes that were watching her.

By now the owner was worried. He didn't like the Shepherd's behaviour. He didn't trust it so he called for his dog to come but as he did so the Shepherd leapt forward and launched an attack. It grabbed the Shih Tzu by the neck and chest and shook her and threw her in the air. Her owner was there in an instant and beat the Shepherd, and although he risked serious injury to himself he was convinced that his dog's injuries would have been much more severe if he had not done so. The attacker ran away and the owner picked up his dog and ran the short distance to the clinic.

His description of the attack eliminated many of the 'justifiable' causes of dog fights. Sex and territory are two understandable causes of dog fights but in this instance there were many other dogs in the vicinity and there were no signs of competition for sex. His dog was neither a territorial nor a sexual threat.

Dominance is a justifiable cause for dog fights but in dominance fights the aggression is almost ritualised. The attack on his dog was a premeditated and murderous one. It was meant to kill.

Jealousy can result in dogs fighting too, but he had never seen this Shepherd before and there seemed no earthly reason why it should be jealous of his Shih Tzu. No, the attack seemed primitive and basic – the hunter and the hunted – the cougar and the fawn – a basic urge to kill.

All members of the canine family are hunter–killers. Wolves, foxes, coyotes, dingos, they all stalk and hunt their prey and they kill to eat and survive. Stalking, hunting and killing are basic instincts. In breeding dogs we have successfully suppressed this instinct to kill, this murder lust. We have in most instances reduced it to a ritualised level. Dogs will ritually shake their toys 'to death' or will 'stalk' grapes on the floor as my dog does, but with the exception of those bred specifically to have a murder lust, breeds like the Pit Bull Terrier, the instinct to kill has been sufficiently submerged. Sometimes it emerges however, more in some breeds than in others. The dog's primitive instinct to stalk prey and kill becomes irresistible. An urban dog with this overwhelming instinct, a dog that has no 'real' prey to stalk, no mice or rabbits, will use other dogs as scapegoats. Rural dogs will use sheep and lambs, more appropriate animals, especially when you consider the term involved.

Scapegoat games are about the most serious that dogs can play and the scapegoat for the murder lust is not always another dog or a sheep. The dog I described that followed my

EXHIBIT "A"
Wolf in
Poodle's Clothing

son's friend home and attacked him and his mother on their doorstep was such a dog. Greyhounds are primitive enough that they will chase a mechanical rabbit around a track because they want to tear it to shreds. Two retired working greyhounds killed a little girl in Ireland a few years ago as she was carrying her doll, and presumably they wanted to kill that too.

Aggression because of competition or jealousy or even revenge can be understandable in some circumstances but aggression because of a primitive murder lust is not. Dogs that have this type of inexplicable aggression, and use other dogs or cats or people as their scapegoats, can rightly be called canine psychopaths. There are ways to try to modify their behaviour with drugs and with intensive retraining, but anyone who tries to do so should be aware that the probability is high that the dog will act aggressively again and that they should bear full responsibility for it.

OWNER: 'OFF WITH HIS HEAD!'

On Yom Kippur, the Day of Atonement, the priest of the ancient Hebrews, the biblical Jews, placed his hands on the head of a goat and recited the sins of the people and in doing so symbolically transferred all evil to the goat. The goat was then taken from the temple and allowed to escape into the wilderness, taking with it all evil and clearing the community of all sin.

The biblical Jews let their scapegoat escape. Some of my clients don't.

In *Pets and Their People* I told the story of Mr Reilly and the Dobermann he brought in for me to kill. I explained how I discovered, by sheer accident, that he was using the dog to get back at his wife; that the dog was his scapegoat and that his wife was in fact hiding from him in a hostel for battered wives. Pets make ideal scapegoats. They're at the bottom of the pile. If your superior kicks you and you want to kick someone else, ultimately the low man on the totem pole bears the brunt of the fury, except in the situation I'm describing the low man is a dog.

The greatest enigma of pet ownership is that pet owners can say, in one breath, that the dog is their 'best friend' and the next moment withdraw all their 'friend's' privileges and rights. In Chapter Five I discussed Constance Perin's theory on why we can love and hate our pets at the same time, but there are many more reasons why some people use their pets as scapegoats.

One of the commonest reasons is simple retaliation. If a dog

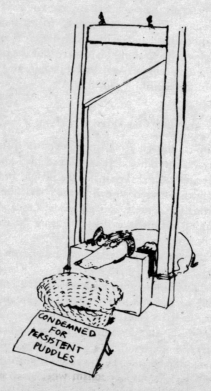

CONDEMNED FOR PERSISTENT PUDDLES

isn't housetrained properly it runs the risk of being abused. If it continues to mess it may well be brought to me for execution. The owner blames the dog but if the dog hasn't been properly housetrained *by the owner* in the first place, then the dog isn't to blame and the owner should recognise that.

People will use animals as scapegoats because of prejudice. The prejudice might be directed at the species itself. If someone hates cats, and there are lots of people who do, then they have little compunction about using them for air rifle target practice, for example. And air pellet injuries are surprisingly common, so common that the British Veterinary Association held a press conference about them.

Animals can be used as scapegoats too because of prejudice against the owners. I can recall one incident in which meat poisoned with slug bait was slipped through a letter box because someone didn't like the sexual preferences of the little dog's two female owners.

Pets can be used as scapegoats in order for someone to gain attention, and once again I recall one dog that I had to treat for a ruptured diaphragm because its owner had kicked it to get his wife's attention. I've also seen animals used as scapegoats for amusement, given LSD and other drugs 'just to see what happens'.

Some owners will be cruel to their pets just to show how tough they are, but in perhaps most situations, and that includes many that I have described, the cruelty occurs because the owner is displacing his anger or hostility at something or someone else on to the pet.

Sometimes the result can be innocuous or even whimsical, as in the case of the man who has named his cat Thatcher and who locks the cat out of his house whenever he is displeased with the Leaderene. The seriousness of scapegoat games escalates, however, and I usually become involved at the castration level.

As I have mentioned, castration games between spouses are symbolic, but there is no symbolism when they involve the

male family pet. Male dogs are presented to me by their
female owners for the flimsiest of reasons, starting with
'because he's male'. They might be brought in because the
owner is presenting a show of power or because of prejudice or
because of a feeling of hostility against male humans rather
than for the acceptable reasons for castrating a dog.

The ultimate demand that some people make is the death
penalty. That isn't to say that a request for the euthanasia of a
dog is always wrong – in most instances it is a proper and
humane request. It is wrong, however, when the reason for the
request is revenge.

Pet owners also play scapegoat games with their veterinary
surgeons and with other people. Veterinary surgeons usually
know when they haven't been completely accurate with a
diagnosis or comprehensive with a treatment, and I remember
the first time that I was accused of incompetence and *knew*
that the diagnosis and treatment was correct. I felt like I was
being used. I *was* being used. The owner had, for his own
reasons, chosen to do the exact opposite of what I had told
him to do and now I was being used as the scapegoat because
of his anger at himself.

I recently had to give, as I frequently have to, a grave
prognosis. Pickle's owners thought that the reason why their
young spaniel was not eating or moving around much was
that he had injured his hind legs, but the blood tests were
overwhelmingly conclusive. Pickle had an intensely serious
and irreversible disease of his kidneys and although he was
less than two years of age he had a life expectancy of at the
most a few months.

After fifteen years in practice I have learned how to read pet
owners to some degree and usually find what feels like the
right way to bear bad news. Sometimes I hide it for a little
while and release facts a few at a time; in other circumstances
I explain everything immediately and in a forthright manner.
Pickle's owners were a young couple in their late thirties –
children, weekend cottage, job security and all the trappings

of sensibility and common sense. I explained Pickle's condition as I would to a secure and intelligent couple, but the
husband's reaction was explosive. The nicest things that he
said had to do with my professional competence and they
weren't quotes I'd stick on the wall. In his anger he even
managed to bring in what he alleged were my political,
religious and monetary policy beliefs. I was a real scapegoat.

The scapegoat will see you now, Mrs Perkins

Back in the good old days the bearer of bad news might
have been put to death. Displacing anger on to that person
can be a normal reaction. It can just become excessive
sometimes. Pickle's owners went off for a second opinion and
had the integrity and the grit to come back after the diagnosis
had been confirmed elsewhere. Pickles was eventually put
down but I had felt the full brunt of being a scapegoat.

Although the veterinary surgeon, as the bearer of bad news,
runs a great risk of being made a scapegoat, pet owners can

lash out at others too. I have a client who lets his dogs run
loose who has physically attacked the driver of the car that hit
his dog. It isn't always the driver's fault when there is a road
traffic accident. The owner has to let the dog run the risk in
the first place.

In the late 1950s a journalist named Richard Joseph let his
dog run loose and heard it being hit by a car. His anger at the
car driver prompted him to write a letter to the editor of his
local paper and I'll quote it in full because I think it's a good
letter that is due for re-airing. From the letter it appears that it
probably was the driver's fault, but I can't help but feel that
Joseph felt guilty too for letting his inexperienced dog run on
to the road and that part of his anger was displaced anger –
that the driver was, at least in a small sense, a scapegoat for
his own feeling of anger at himself for letting his dog die in
such a way.

TO THE MAN WHO KILLED MY DOG

I hope you were going somewhere important when you
drove so fast down Cross Highway across Bayberry
Lane, on Tuesday night.

I hope that when you got there the time you saved by
speeding meant something to you or somebody else.

Maybe we'd feel better if we could imagine that you
were a doctor rushing to deliver a baby or ease
somebody's pain. The life of our dog to shorten someone's suffering – that mightn't have been so bad.

But even though all we saw of you was the black
shadow of your car and its jumping red tail lights as you
roared down the road, we know too much about you to
believe it.

You saw the dog, you stepped on your brakes, you felt
the thump, you heard the yelp and then my wife's
scream. Your reflexes are better than your heart and
stronger then your courage – we know that – because

you jumped on the gas again and got out of there as fast as your car could carry you.

Whoever you are, mister, and whatever you do for a living, we know you are a killer.

And in your hands, driving the way you drove on Tuesday night, your car is a murder weapon.

You didn't bother to look, so I'll tell you what the thump and the yelp were. They were Vicky, a six-month-old Basset puppy; white with brown and black markings. An aristocrat, with twelve champions among her fore-bears; but she clowned and she chased, and she loved people and kids and other dogs as much as any mongrel on earth.

I'm sorry you didn't stick around to see the job you did, though a dying dog by the side of the road isn't a very pretty sight. In less than two seconds you and that car of yours transformed a living being that had been beautiful, warm, clean, soft and loving into something dirty, ugly, broken and bloody. A poor shocked and mad thing that tried to sink its teeth into the hand it had nuzzled and licked all its life.

I hope to God that when you hit my dog you had for a moment the sick, dead feeling in the throat and down in the stomach that we have known ever since. And that you feel it whenever you think about speeding down a winding country road again.

Because the next time some eight-year-old boy might be wobbling along on his first bicycle. Or a very little one might wander out past the gate and into the road in the moment it takes a father to bend down to pull a weed out of the drive, the way my pup got away from me.

Or maybe you'll be really lucky again, and only kill another dog, and break the heart of another family.

Richard Joseph
Westport, Connecticut

CHAPTER SEVEN

Clinical Games

1. PSYCHOSOMATIC GAMES

PET: 'I'M SO FRUSTRATED'

Clinical games are games that pets and pet owners play in which the veterinary surgeon frequently becomes enmeshed and is called upon to play an active role. The role varies with the game. In some circumstances the veterinary surgeon is used as a pawn but in other circumstances the games call for him to be a decision maker.

When you see pets and their owners from morning until

evening each day, and listen to what the owners have to tell you, with time your perspective of normal human and animal behaviour probably becomes skewed. If a pet owner comes in and tells you that Fido their Basset Hound looks pale and you take it literally, you've either been eating strange mushrooms, overworking, going to too many Speilberg films or have become a romantic fantasist. But if you fail to pay attention to what the owner is *trying* to tell you, you might be missing the most important point in the medical history taking. To appreciate clinical games the veterinary surgeon has to understand the intensity of the relationship some pet owners have with their pets.

My assistant veterinary surgeon, through my error, failed to arrive one Friday morning when I had arranged to spend the day at the library and my nurses contacted me to get me back to the clinic. By the time I arrived there was almost an hour's backlog of patients and clients in the reception room, but for a moment I saw veterinary medicine from the outside looking in, from my clients' perspective.

I recently moved my practice into a 175-year-old building in a row of impeccably maintained Georgian shops near Marble Arch in London, and converted the front of the shop into the reception room. I restored the original fireplace in that room and renovated as much of the fabric of the interior as could be done, choosing not to put up any curtains on the floor to ceiling front window because I was so pleased with the renovation. I didn't want to obstruct the view in any way. But this also meant that as I neared and entered the front door I could watch the goings-on in reception.

A Boxer dog was straining on its lead inquisitively trying to have a sniff at Humphrette, my reception room African grey parrot. Humphrette was undoubtedly meowing. A German Shepherd was pacing back and forth on a short lead, its ears flattened back and its eyes pleading, stopping every few seconds to put its front paws on its owner, trying for all its worth to climb up on to its owner's lap. There was a closed whicker basket, moving in front of the reception desk. A paw reached out of the small side window of the basket and with claws extended, waved and then retracted. A Springer Spaniel lay at his owner's feet asleep, oblivious to everything. Looking into that room from the outside rather than from the inside gave me a completely different perspective. It was a madhouse and the keeper was returning.

It had never entered my mind that it is the circus-like quality of veterinary work that is so satisfying. Out of the anarchy of the reception room, each animal and owner is filtered through a door into the relative calm of the examining room, where the animal is attended to and the owner is talked to. A diagnosis of a problem is made, treatment is given, the owner is instructed and then the calm ends. The dog pulls the owner back to reception with a tenacity equal to that of Old Buck when he pulled a half-ton sleigh for his owner in *The Call of the Wild* – straining every sinew – concentrating every effort – superhuman if only they were.

Of all the clinical games that are played, the ones that have the greatest circus-like qualities are the psychosomatic games. Psychosomatic illnesses do occur in dogs and cats. We are not the only species with the ability to create them. Compulsive eating, sympathy lameness, diarrhoea, asthma-like conditions and even epilepsy in dogs can in some cases be psychosomatic, and in many if not most of these cases the game is played because the pet is frustrated.

Virginia and Paul Smith got married, got a dog, had a baby and ended up among my most frequent visitors. Their Gordon Setter Angus is as good and even-tempered a four-year-old dog as you would ever want. He is affectionate, enjoys playing with other dogs and meeting people, isn't destructive in any way and never excessively begs attention. He could even be described as emotionally nondescript if it did not paint such a pejorative picture. Angus has always been a pleasure to see

Tell the dog to get undressed and lie down, would you nurse?

because he is so laid back and relaxed, but shortly after the Smiths' baby was born, Angus's owners were in because he developed a sore area on the top of his front paw. Angus had started licking his paw when the baby arrived home and had licked away the fur, causing quite a sore. Angus had a skin problem given many names – lick dermatitis and lick granuloma are the two most common – and the problem is very difficult to overcome. It's difficult to overcome because it's really a psychosomatic illness. The dog is playing 'I'm so frustrated'.

Psychosomatic games involve a change in the behaviour of the pet and a change in the pet's chemistry. It really doesn't matter which comes first (don't forget, from an egg's perspective, a chicken is just an intermediate stage between two eggs), pragmatically speaking if both occur your pet can have a psychosomatic problem.

With pets, a change in the *owner's* behaviour can also lead to a change in the pet's chemistry. That's why tender loving care is so important in proper nursing. Some scientists say that tender loving care somehow stimulates the chemistry of the patient's own pain-killing system. They have observed that the placebo effect – making people feel better by telling them that they are being given a potent drug whereas in fact they are only being given sugar tablets – works with thirty per cent of patients. But they have also observed that if the placebo is given with enthusiasm it can work in up to seventy per cent of patients. The behaviour of the people who care for the patient affects the chemistry of the patient and it doesn't matter whether the patient is human or canine.

Angus had a classic problem. For almost four years he had been an 'only child'. All the parenting attention had been given to him. He had never been obsessive about it and probably just accepted it as natural. But the status quo changed when the baby arrived. The Smiths had done what I suggested they do when the baby arrived and they had not changed Angus's routine, but the inevitable changes in the household bore fruit in Angus's front left paw. Treating the problem with cortisone would give temporary relief but Angus was brought back every few months for further treatment.

There are dozens of treatments recorded for Angus's problem – applying creams, injecting the sore with cortisone, bandaging it, freezing it with ultracold therapy, surgically removing it or having the dog wear a plastic Elizabethan collar that prevents him from physically licking the sore – but all that these treatments do is treat the effect. None of them get at the cause because that's in Angus's mind.

Psychosomatic games aren't played just by dogs that get smothered rather than mothered. Psychosomatic games can be played by any dog or cat but we frequently don't even recognise them. The dog that 'pines' when it is separated from its owners either through kennelling or through hospitalisation can be described as playing a psychosmatic game which in human terms would be called anorexia nervosa. There cannot be a veterinary surgeon in practice who has not hospitalised a dog or cat, become concerned over the animal's unwillingness to eat while hospitalised regardless of what it is offered, and released it to its home where its appetite is miraculously restored.

Most pet owners, eighty-one per cent to be precise, feel that their pets are tuned in to the feelings of family members and can show their anxiety over family matters by having diarrhoea, by vomiting or by appearing depressed or otherwise behaving differently to normal. I have seen a Dalmatian viciously chew its hind leg (in an area that had previously been physically damaged) when his owners had a marital tiff, a German Shepherd have diarrhoea whenever it was separated from his master, a Cavalier King Charles drink massive quantities of water for five days each time it returned home from the kennels and a Pointer develop a non-existent lameness in a previously injured leg whenever there was unusual activity in the house.

When I first started practising veterinary medicine I didn't believe that psychosomatic illness could occur in any species other than the human, but the longer I practise the more I come to appreciate that psychosomatic games are surprisingly common among pets and are played with adroitness and skill.

OWNER: 'EXAMINE HIM AGAIN. I *KNOW* THERE'S SOMETHING WRONG'

Timmy had a heart attack last week, cancer of the liver the month before, picked up a virus infection a short while before that when he was brought to the clinic to have his nails cut, and right now has feline leukemia. Timmy's owner knows he has feline leukemia because she heard about the disease on a radio programme and a cat was in their back garden the week before. The fact that Timmy is a dog and not a cat and that the disease can only occur in cats is irrelevant. Timmy's owner *knows* that he has it and science is wrong to even suggest that dogs can't get it. 'Why shouldn't dogs be able to get it?' she says.

All of us at the clinic feel sorry for Timmy because we know he's a pawn in a game. He's not treated as a dog, he's treated as a little fur person. We know that we are pawns too; that his owner has what can only be called a pathological attachment for this fat little chihuahua. We've tried to change things but so far have been unsuccessful. Trying to talk to Timmy's owner is like trying to box with a marshmallow. Every statement, every punch, goes unheeded, gets lost in the vapours. Timmy's owner is on another wavelength. We've been telling her for years that Timmy is a tough healthy little guy and she's never heard a word.

Timmy is her religious leader, her film star, her war hero. He's her idol and as sure as the full moon returns every month so does Timmy's owner, convinced deep in her being that he has an incurable disease. And each month the dog apologetically looks up from the examining table at me and seems to say, 'I'm sorry to be such a nuisance' and I despair that he has such a miserable life.

Timmy is never – never – allowed to meet other dogs. 'They're so dirty!' On one occasion, his owner brought her own disinfectant to clean my examining table because she had been unhappy with the way the previous month I had removed all traces of the animal I had examined before Timmy. I doubt that he has ever been off his lead. He is never allowed to act like a dog but he is still worshipped, adulated, fretted over and worried about. There is no good and bad about him. There is nothing harmful about him only things harmful to him. And 'things' are always harming him. 'Examine him again, Dr Fogle. I *know* there is something seriously wrong.'

Some people have an overwhelming ability to love and to suffer intensely for every living creature. I am constantly being brought dying pigeons to mend or to put out of their

misery, and it isn't only the furred and feathered that are capable of invoking that response. My brother gave up fishing almost thirty years ago because he found it unpleasant to inflict the coup de grace on his catch. My mother and sister never fished because they felt sorry for the creatures finding themselves caught and struggling on a line. (My father and I, on the other hand, might have felt those feelings but fished like herons nevertheless.) The veterinarian in the State of Washington, however, who was brought a decapitated ant and asked to repair it was in the presence of a Timmy-owner in extremis and it can reasonably be argued that zealous 'overcarers' have an inner need for that kind of care for themselves.

Timmy's owner is an extreme example of the owner who is convinced that there is some serious medical problem with his or her pet, but there are others who play less overwhelming variations of the game. I once went on a house visit to examine a psychoanalyst's cat and as I reached under the dining-room table to pick up the animal, her owner said, 'Stop! She doesn't want to be picked up.' The cat was showing no resentment and no fear at what I was doing so I asked the owner how she knew her cat didn't want to be picked up. 'She told me before you arrived,' came the reply. 'We understand each other perfectly and she told me she wanted me to pick her up for you.' So she did and I examined her cat!

Pet owners impute all kinds of behaviour and thoughts to their pets. Dr Alan Beck at the University of Pennsylvania says, 'Ninety-nine per cent of people admit talking to their dogs and the other one per cent are probably lying.' People confide in their pets. They do so because dogs and cats send us back uncomplicated signals – a woof or meow or tweet is interpreted by the owner as happiness or anger or excitement or joy but rarely as anything more sophisticated. Pets evoke the lost childhood in us when the grass was greener, the sky was bluer, when problems were black and white, when there were answers to everything.

Pet owners who care for their pets sufficiently to take them to their veterinary surgeon for medical attention do so either because they feel a moral obligation to do so or because of their emotional attachment to their animal, and it is this latter group that plays a distinct variation of psychosomatic games – 'ticket of admission' games.

Both the pet and the vet are pawns in ticket of admission games, which are based on the pet owner's perception of the veterinary surgeon. Several years ago a survey was conducted among the British. 'Who do you trust the most?' they were asked. 'Your doctor, dentist, solicitor, minister, MP, veterinary surgeon?' In that survey veterinary surgeons were far and away the most popular professionals in England. That was their image among the general public and it is probably the same or even more so among pet owners.

The general image of the veterinary surgeon is of an honest, no-nonsense person, practical and pragmatic but with gentle hands and a compassionate disposition. The pet owner's image of him is as someone who can tell what's wrong with their pet even though the animal can't talk and in comparison they will sometimes say, 'When I went to see my own doctor I even told him what was wrong with me and he still couldn't make the right diagnosis.' They see their vets as uncomplicated people with good basketside manners. It's a fantasy image which is in part preconceived because of their own

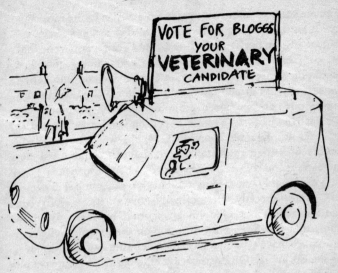

relationships with their pets. It has also to some extent developed because of the remoteness that many people feel from their doctors. They feel that doctors treat people like cattle and that veterinary surgeons treat cattle like people. Or, as one woman once wrote, '"Steady, old girl" and a sympathetic hand on the udder is appreciated by nervous ruminants of all species.'

A ticket of admission game can only be played if the pet owner has at least in part this image of the veterinary surgeon, because in this game the pet owner uses the pet as a method of gaining access to a sympathetic professional, or to be more precise, to someone they think of as a sympathetic professional.

Sometimes what the ticket of admission player wants to do is to talk about something totally unconnected with the pet. That can often be something of a medical nature since they see their veterinary surgeon as medically knowledgeable but also approachable. When a psychiatrist, Michael McCulloch, explained this to me I had a guarded attitude to the idea, but once I started paying more attention to the 'non-veterinary' content of practice it almost instantly became apparent that he was correct. Within weeks of his explaining ticket of admission games to me, a middle-aged woman who I had known for years brought her dog in for me to clip its nails and during our conversation she almost abruptly explained that her husband had had a minor operation two weeks before and had still not regained consciousness. She was a retiring lady and even in the circumstances felt that she couldn't ask her husband's doctor, so she asked me. 'What happened?'

It is probably more common that ticket of admission games will either directly or indirectly involve the pet. When someone says to me, 'Fido means more to me than anyone,' I know that they are saying it to me on the assumption that I am 'safe', that I will understand. When someone else says just as she is leaving, 'Oh, by the way, Fido has tried to bite people but my husband won't do anything to stop him,' I know that the owner wants advice on the social side of the problem not just the medical side.

Ticket of admission games get more personal and more intimate when they involve the physical health of the pet owners, and there seems to be one specific area of medicine where pet owners credit their veterinary surgeons – skin disease. I'm frequently shown pimples and pustules, inflammations and irritations on owners and asked to pass judgement. On a hot day last summer a young woman brought her cat in because it was scratching and when I had examined it I explained to her that her cat had fleas. 'Do they bite us?' she asked and when I answered in the affirmative, in a flash, if you'll pardon the term, she whipped her T-shirt up to her shoulders and asked, 'Are these flea bites?' That might seem like an uncomplicated question and in other circumstances, an ankle or an arm for example, I have a good close look and say yes or no. Under those circumstances, however, and from what I remember from my Boy Scout manual on the female anatomy, there was no way they could be classified as flea bites. The story does however say something about the attitude of some pet owners to their veterinary surgeons. In ticket of admission games the pet owner sees the veterinary surgeon as trustworthy and understanding, someone to confide in, a feeling of confidence most necessary with the games I will describe in the final section of this book.

2. END GAMES

PET: 'I'M NOT AFRAID'

When my Golden Retriever Honey was about fifteen years old she gave up going to parties. When she was younger she greeted each person at the door, then spent the evening strategically placed in the epicentre of the living room eyeing all activity and responding to every wink and gesture. Eye to eye contact for a fraction of a millisecond was all that was needed to stimulate her to amble over to the person whose attention she had caught for a pat on her head or a few sweet nothings whispered in her ear.

A year or so before that, she had given up her unpaid position of office manager and dogsbody for me. In her own benign way she had helped build up my practice. She chose her work herself but carried it out with a seriousness and a dignity that her successor, who thinks that she's a clown and that life's a riot, will never have.

From late June until early September each year Honey carefully positioned herself on the pavement outside my clinic from morning to late afternoon. She lay there as solemn as a cigar store Indian, alerting the neighbourhood to the fact that there was a new veterinary surgeon in the area. Every so often she was enchanted by the aroma of a passer-by, perhaps they had something dug up in their pockets, and she would get up and wag a hello and have a good sniff, but otherwise she was as stoic as Churchill's statue in front of Westminster. At lunchtime I would take her to Hyde Park where she greeted

every dog owner, distributed my cards, retrieved her tennis ball until I collapsed from throwing it, and then went for a dog paddle in the Serpentine.

Honey spent her winter days ensconced like a dowager duchess on the one comfortable chair in my reception room. She'd curl up on it and from her throne, and with eyes as alert as a Golden Retriever's can be, she would peruse the scene and watch the competition come and go. Sometimes nasties would be brought in, but if one of them tried to intimidate her she just turned her head away as if to say 'You're disgusting!' and during her entire life she was never bitten by another dog.

She also carried out her managerial duties just outside my office door and beside my desk. She'd lie in these places and watch the activity so that by the time she was ten years old she could diagnose ninety per cent of the ailments she saw. Honey was secure in her position. Each day she went outside and had a good sniff of the marks left by the opposition but she knew that no matter how many dogs and cats entered her territory she had no reason to be afraid. The status quo never changed. Her place was always secure.

Eventually Honey reached retirement age. It was her own decision although we played a part in it. Honey decided to give up practice management as a career and we decided that her lying out on the pavement would also have to end. She had a few strokes in her early teens and although she rapidly recovered from each of them, one summer day we saw her lie down outside in the gutter instead of against the railings. She did so with aplomb but it was a pretty dumb thing to do, and that was when my wife and I realised that we now had more responsibilities in looking after her.

It was in early retirement that Honey also gave up partying. When she and the children were younger she mixed into everything. We really hadn't realised how insidiously she mixed until we looked at old pictures of the children's birthday parties. Honey was in each picture, looking solemn as she always did. We're a reasonably enlightened family but we still thought of her as a member of it.

Honey gently geared her activity down as the years progressed. For most of her life play was the most important thing – more important than food – and her happiest ritual game remained a ride in the car. In her early life she was driven to Kensington Gardens each day for her exercise and from that time on she always equated car rides with fun. Now in her declining years, she pleaded with her eyes to come with us whenever she saw us getting ready to go somewhere in the car, but when we took her she was content to just fall asleep and dream geriatric dreams, like chasing lame rabbits.

As with many individuals who reach retirement she still wanted to do some work, so I hired her as a part-time promoter for a mobile animal clinic that I was setting up. I bought a small camper van with large picture windows on each side and converted the interior to include an examining table, drug cabinets and oxygen and anaesthetic equipment. There were long wide seats beneath the picture windows and

Honey would spend her day lying on these seats with her head on the bolster, her body up at the chest level of passers-by. Still solemn, still dignified, still silly.

There comes a time, however, when a pet gets older when the pendulum swings and having that pet is no longer fun but is instead an obligation. That happened with Honey when she was about sixteen years old. Insidiously, circumstances changed. It started innocuously enough when she developed an obsession for food. At first I attributed this to a three-month episode when she was fourteen years old when I had to treat her for a rare disease with massive amounts of daily cortisone. I thought the cortisone was the only cause of her food craze but it wasn't. Old age was and with time she got to the stage where she demanded to be fed. She had gone deaf when she was about twelve and at that time readily learned to obey hand signals, but because she was deaf she didn't know what she sounded like when she barked and when she barked for food she sounded like a mouse.

Honey slept in a basket in our bedroom. Spring came once more and she seemed to sleep all day and to pant all night. She wasn't afraid of growing old and she did so gently and with grace, but now we were getting afraid. The weather got more humid and her nighttime panting got louder, reverberating through the whole house. It became our normal background noise and whenever it stopped Julia and I would both sit bolt upright in bed and stare at her basket. 'Is she dead? Hell! No!'

There's no cure for old age in pets nor should there be. Pet owners can suffer when a dog or cat nears the end of its natural existence because they are afraid that the pet might be suffering, afraid that it might not be enjoying life, afraid that they will be losing a good companion. But a pet isn't afraid of death. Sure, old dogs don't like surprises and they often want to be left alone but dogs and cats aren't afraid of death the way their owners often are. Literature is full of stories and parables of animals taking themselves off to die with dignity.

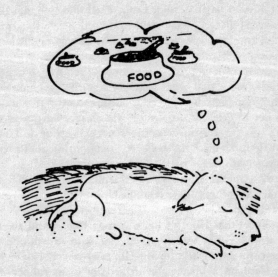

When Honey finally died late that spring it was with my help. She died without suffering and without being afraid. Her owners had a harder time.

Owner: 'She Was My Best Friend'

We all knew for some time that Honey was soon going to die and I knew that I was going to have to be actively involved. Every six months for her last few years I had done complete blood profile examinations and knew that, regrettably, everything inside her was working perfectly. It was her weak hind legs and her strokes that would precipitate my decision to end her life.

Veterinary surgeons are used to giving bad news and I knew all the ploys that pet owners use to deny the news, so I

couldn't use them myself. People will often act as if they
haven't heard what I've said. I might tell someone that their
pet has heart disease, bone cancer and a degenerative spinal
condition and the owner will respond by asking me to cut the
pet's nails.

The death of a pet can be traumatic because sometimes
the relationship that you have with a pet is unique –
different from any human relationship. There is not and
should not be grief for the loss of 'what might have been', as
there is when a person dies before maturity, but as I have
explained throughout the book the relationship that people
can have with their pets is more complicated than it
outwardly appears. It can also be an intense relationship and
the suffering when that relationship ends can be more
traumatic than expected.

Julia knew that Honey's life was soon to end and she did
things to make that transition easy for both herself and the
dog. In early spring she rebuilt Honey's basket. Honey had
always slept on a blanket on a piece of foam rubber in a

whicker basket but now Julia converted the basket into a veritable cloud. She padded it with wadding, stapled it firm and made a bed that was so cosy and friendly that my younger children wanted to get in it. Honey loved it. The first time she used it she snored non-stop for fourteen hours.

But it was equally or even more important for Julia. She had a need to feel needed and to do something. I could give the old dog the odd injection of vitamins or body-building hormone but Julia felt helpless with Honey's impending death and building the cloud was fulfilling a need.

Eugene O'Neill felt the same need when his dog Blemie was dying. The O'Neills' relationship with Blemie was a close one. O'Neill's wife Carlotta had once said, 'Gene and I spoil him no end but always say he is the only one of our children who has not disillusioned us.' O'Neill did what he could do best and to comfort both his wife and himself he wrote Blemie's will.

WILL

I Silverdene Emblem O'Neill (familiarly known as Blemie), because the burden of my years and infirmities is heavy upon me, and I realise the end of my life is near, do hereby bury my last will and testament in the mind of my master. He will not know it is there until after I am dead. Then, remembering me in his loneliness, he will suddenly know of this testament, and I ask him to inscribe it as a memorial to me.

I have little in the way of material things to leave. Dogs are wiser than men. They do not waste their days hoarding property. They do not ruin their sleep worrying about how to keep the objects they have not. There is nothing of value I have to bequeath except my love and my faith. These I leave to all those who have loved me, to my master and mistress, who I know will mourn me most . . . Perhaps it is vain of me to boast when I am so near death, which returns all beasts and vanities to dust, but I have always been an extremely lovable dog.

I ask my master and mistress to remember me always, but not to grieve for me too long. In my life I have tried to be a comfort to them in time of sorrow, and a reason for added joy in their happiness. It is painful for me to think that even in death I should cause them pain. Let them remember that while no dog has had a happier life (and this I owe to their love and care for me), now that I have grown blind and deaf and lame, and even my sense of smell fails me so that a rabbit could be right under my nose and I might not know, my pride is sunk to a sick, bewildered humiliation. I feel life is taunting me with having over-lingered my welcome. It is time I said goodbye, before I become too sick a burden on myself and those who love me. It will be a sorrow to leave them, but not a sorrow to die. Dogs do not fear death as men do. We accept it as part of life, not as something alien and terrible which destroys life. What may come after death, who knows? I would like to believe with those of my fellow Dalmatians who are devout Mohammedans, that there is a Paradise where one is always young and full-bladdered; where all the day one dallies and dillies with an amorous multitude of houris, beautifully spotted . . .

I am afraid this is too much for even such a dog as I am to expect. But peace, at least, is certain. Peace and long rest for weary old heart and head and limbs, and eternal sleep in the earth I loved so well. Perhaps, after all, this is best. One last request I earnestly make. I have heard my mistress say, 'When Blemie dies we must never have another dog. I love him so much I could never love another one.' Now I would ask her, for love of me, to have another. It would be a poor tribute to my memory never to have a dog again. What I would like is that, having once had me in the family, now she cannot live without a dog . . . To him I bequeath my collar and leash

and my overcoat and raincoat, made to order in 1929 at Hermes in Paris. He can never wear them with the distinction I did, walking around the Place Vendôme, or later along Park Avenue, all eyes fixed on me in admiration, but again I am sure he will do his utmost not to appear a mere gauche provincial dog . . . One last word of farewell, dear master and mistress. Whenever you visit my grave, say to yourselves with regret but also happiness in your hearts at the remembrance of my long happy life with you: 'Here lies one who loved us and whom we loved.' No matter how deep my sleep I shall hear you, and not all the power of death can keep my spirit from wagging a grateful tail.

It was the first Thursday in June when I knew that my dog's life should end. On Wednesday she had eaten and slept and had a roll on the floor and greeted the children when they came home from school as she always did, but on Thursday morning I could see in her eyes that she had had another stroke. She had difficulty getting up and she looked worried. I would have done it then but Julia was taping a TV play in Birmingham, so I made the dog comfortable and left her in her basket but went downstairs to my office, filled a syringe with the barbiturate concentrate I would use and brought that back up and left it in a drawer near her.

Julia returned to London the next morning and came directly to our youngest daughter's sports day at the school playground. I guess she could read my face and she knew I had decided that Honey's life must end, and she agreed. With the exception of the times I had carried the dog outside to relieve herself she hadn't left her basket during the previous twenty-four hours, and when we got back home she thumped a hello with her tail but just lay there sphinx-like looking apologetic. Julia kissed her on her head and said goodbye and I injected her and she died. We held each other close and we both shed tears.

I had to get back to work – people were waiting downstairs – but Julia was left alone and she dusted and vacuumed and washed and ironed and did other things just to do things.

Julia made a big meal for all of us that evening. After work I brought Humphrette, our parrot, upstairs to the living room and opened his cage so that he could sit on top of it. Julia worked away in the kitchen pretending to be busy but really thinking of nothing but Honey. Honey had originally been her dog and had seen her through all the ups and downs in life. She was there for the ups. We had met when she brought the dog to me when Honey was unwell. And Honey was waiting at home after the birth of each child. But there had been downs before all of that and at one time in Julia's life, when Honey was quite young, the dog had genuinely been her best friend. Honey was a good friend to me too. I had never had a big dog before. My family had always had terriers, either the rape and plunder or comfort-me types. I had never before been able to go for a walk with a dog off a lead and through Honey discovered the pleasure of traipsing off alone, just with a dog. Honey was a new experience and I liked it. And she probably taught me as much about practising veterinary medicine as any human ever did.

I went into the kitchen and Julia put her arms around my neck and sobbed. We stood there for a few minutes, lost in sorrow, arms around one another, but quickly regained our composure and wiped away the tears when we heard a strange 'hello' from the hallway. Humphrette's timing was perfect! She waddled into the kitchen over to our feet and this time said it more mellifluously, 'Hellllllllo.'

That evening I took Honey's body wrapped in a sheet, and her basket downstairs and left them in my office. Julia and I made small talk and eventually went to bed, but I couldn't get to sleep. I lay there watching the numbers change on my clock thinking about the dog and my family. I was in a different country because of her. My children were my children because of her. She had been the seedcorn for a complete change in the path I always thought my life would take. At two in the morning, still sleepless, I quietly got out of bed and went downstairs and sat down at my desk. Orange light from the sodium street lamp outside the window filtered through the room and I looked at Honey's basket and wrapped body and thought about the years she had spent lying on that floor, such a good companion.

I didn't know what to think. The next day we were taking her a great distance to bury her in the grounds of a friend's house. A chapter of my life was ending and I didn't particularly want it to end. I sat there in the room where I had spent most of my last decade, and then I remembered that I had a clipping somewhere in my files that I suddenly wanted to read. I searched through my filing cabinet and finally found it, an editorial from an Ontario newspaper, written at the turn of the century in answer to a subscriber's question, 'Where shall I bury my dog?' I remembered that when I first read it I was amused by the florid Victorian prose and by the gushing sentimentality, but now by the soft light coming through the window from the street lamp I read it again.

We would say to the Ontario man that there are various places in which a dog may be buried. We are thinking now of a setter, whose coat was flame in the sunshine, and who, so far as we are aware, never entertained a mean or an unworthy thought. This setter is buried beneath a cherry tree, under four feet of garden loam, and at its proper season the cherry strews petals on the green lawn of his grave. Beneath a cherry tree, or an apple; or any flowering shrub is an excellent place to bury a dog. Beneath such trees, such shrubs, he slept in the drowsy summer, or gnawed at a flavorous bone, or lifted his head to challenge some strange intruder. These are good places in life or in death. Yet it is a small matter, for if the dog be well remembered, if sometimes he leaps through your dreams actual as in life, eyes kindling, laughing, begging it matters not at all where that dog sleeps. On a hill where the wind is unrebuked, and the trees are roaring, or beside a stream he knew in puppyhood, or somewhere in the flatness of a pasture lane where some exhilarating cattle grazed, is all one to the dog, and all one to you – and nothing is gained, nothing is lost – if memory lives.

But there is one place to bury a dog. If you bury him in this spot, he will come to you when you call – come to you over the grim, dim frontiers of death and down the well-remembered path and to your side again. And though you call a dozen living dogs to heel they shall not growl at him, nor resent his coming, for he belongs there. People may scoff at you who see no slightest blade of grass bent by his footfall, who hear no whimper, people who never really had a dog. Smile at them, for you shall know something that is hidden from them, and which is well worth knowing. The one best place to bury a good dog is in the heart of his master.

We buried Honey the next day under a giant sycamore tree. We broke up her basket and buried that with her too. Somehow that was one of the most satisfying things we did. None of us at that time could face the thought of just throwing it out. It was the one thing she had had since she was a pup and it had been her security whenever a raincloud came into her life. Burying her in her basket was a symbolic gesture that helped us to cope with the loss of such a good friend.

Over the next few days we had to adjust to many changes to the routine of the last sixteen years. We couldn't bear the thought of another dog – a strange dog – living in the house, living in Honey's house, and we all decided that we'd wait the six months until around Christmas and then start thinking about getting another pet, but the mind is a magnificent piece of chemistry that over the millenia has developed its own inbuilt ways of accepting death. Four weeks later we were the happy and contented owners of Liberty Olympia Sweetpea Chewingdog Fogle.

SUGGESTED FURTHER READING

Two excellent books on dog training are:

The Monks of New Skete, *How to be Your Dog's Best Friend: A Training Manual for Dog Owners*, Little Brown & Co., Boston, 1978

Kay White and J. M. Evans, MRCVS, *How to Have a Well Mannered Dog*, Paperfronts, Elliot Right Way Books, Kingswood, Surrey

Two excellent books on general human behaviour are:

Eric Berne, *Games People Play: The Psychology of Human Relationships*, Penguin Books Ltd, London, 1970

John Bowlby, *Attachment and Loss*, Basic Books Inc., New York, 1969

Two books that quite specifically describe the ins and outs of pet owning are:

Bruce Fogle, *Pets and Their People*, Sphere Books, London, 1986

Herbert A. Nieberg & Arlene Fischer, *Pet Loss: A Thoughtful Guide for Adults and Children*, Harper & Row, London, 1984

If you are interested in the scientific research that has been published in the field of people–pet relations, there are three textbooks:

R. Anderson, B. Hart & L. Hart (eds.), *The Pet Connection: Its Influence on Our Health and Quality of Life*, University of Minnesota Press, Minneapolis, Minnesota, 1984

Bruce Fogle (ed.), *Interrelations Between People and Pets*, Charles Thomas, Springfield, Illinois, 1981

A. Katcher & A. Beck (eds.), *New Perspectives on Our Lives with Companion Animals*, University of Pennsylvania Press, Philadelphia, Pennsylvania, 1983

INDEX

GRACE McHATTIE
Problem Puss

Does your cat scratch the furniture, eat your plants, bite you, eat too much or too little?

Cats have special emotional, physical and intellectual needs and it is important for their owners to understand their spoken and body language, likes and dislikes.

In this fascinating and informative book, the author, an expert on cat behaviour, explains the origin and treatment of problems from the most common ones of soiling and scratching to the more unusual such as sucking clothes, jealousy and bald spots. She also tells how to train your cat so that problems never arise.

Grace McHattie, is the editor of *Cat World* and lives near Brighton with her four cats.

GRACE McHATTIE
The Cat Maintenance Manual
200 Tips for Owners

Do you want a painless and foolproof way of administering pills to your cat? Do you know which plants in your garden are poisonous to cats? Do you know why you should ask a friend to walk through your house when you're away on holiday in order to control cat fleas?

The answers to these questions, and many more tips and hints for cat-owners on every subject from health, feeding and grooming to travelling, house-training and preventing your cat from scratching the furniture or catching birds, are found in this unique and invaluable book.

Delightfully illustrated by John Mansbridge, this is a book in which everyone from the first-time cat-owner to the most experienced will find something useful and intriguing.

GRACE McHATTIE
The Cat Maintenance Log Book

A companion volume, in diary form, to *The Cat Maintenance Manual*.

This unique book gives invaluable topical tips, advice and warnings on cat care throughout the year. In the form of a diary (with dates but no days, so that it can be used for any or several years), with plenty of space for recording events or appointments in your or your cat's life, there are also fill-in sections for veterinary, inoculation and worming records and for keeping a loving record of your cat in years to come.

Beautifully illustrated throughout, this is a must for every cat-lover.

DAVID GREENE
Incredible Cats
The Secret Powers of Your Pet

Every cat, from the humble tabby to the rare Persian, is
capable of mental, physical and even extrasensory feats unique in the animal kingdom. During ten years of worldwide
investigation, the author has talked to both pet owners and
researchers to discover not only what cats can achieve but
how science attempts to explain their powers. The portrait
which emerges of this well-loved family pet is far stronger
and more intriguing than the fondest owner could imagine.

David Greene is a research and consultant psychologist and
lives in Eastbourne, Sussex

JILLY COOPER
Intelligent and Loyal
A Celebration of the Mongrel

'What breed are they?' she said, looking at our dogs.
'Mongrels!' I said.
She drew back in horror, then remembered her manners and said lamely, 'Well, they're supposed to be *awfully* intelligent and loyal, aren't they?'

Mongrels, 'bitser' dogs, cross-breeds: there are more than 150 million of them in the world today. Mongrels are frequently loyal and entertaining companions to millions of people. Why is it that all the books concentrate on pedigree dogs?

In *Intelligent and Loyal* Jilly Cooper has redressed the balance by writing a tribute to all Britain's mongrels – and by extension to all the mongrels of the world – and of the place they occupy in our heads and homes. Her collaborators in this enterprise have been hundreds of mongrel owners who wrote about their loved ones and the photographer Graham Wood who has captured many aspects of mongrel life in pictures. Out of this emerges a fascinating, moving and often composite portrait.

Intelligent and Loyal offers readers a verbal and pictorial classification for their mongrels so that they can tell at a glance if their dog is a Vertical Shagpile, a Borderline Collie, or a Bertrand Russell. And it offers a delightful and eloquent celebration of the exploits in love, in war, at home and abroad of creatures whose eyes and gestures may speak volumes but who have had to wait patiently for this book to chronicle in words and pictures their natures and their lives in rich diversity.

Photographs by Graham Wood.

NORMAN THELWELL
Top Dog
The Complete Canine Compendium

As every experienced dog-owner knows, man's best friend is a complex bundle of appetites, instincts and winsome wiles. Few first-time pet-owners will realise, however, just what a responsibility they are taking on. So Thelwell – probably the most celebrated and popular cartoonist in Britain today – has kindly provided them with this invaluable handbook full of advice on choosing, training, feeding, exercising and caring for our four-legged friends. It also emphasises the importance of protecting one's own interests – not to mention those of one's neighbours – for an ill-trained hound will soon develop a healthy disrespect for law and order. Here is a superb collection designed to give every dog-owner a new leash of life in the canine world.